BOAZ ON BUSINESS

Building Multi-Generational
Wealth During Chaotic Times

Jeffery S. Watson
With **Eddie Speed, Kira Golden**
and **Rob Anspach**

BOAZ ON BUSINESS
Building Multi-Generational
Wealth During Chaotic Times

Copyright © 2024 Jeffery S. Watson
Produced by: Anspach Media
Cover design by: Freddy Solis
Editing & Direction: Debbie DiPolito

ISBN 13: 979-8-9889988-8-4

Printed in USA

Disclaimer: This book is designed to give the reader general information on the subjects contained herein. It is offered with the understanding that the authors and publisher do not guarantee any specific future results. The authors are not rendering professional advice on specific facts or matters and, accordingly, assume no liability whatsoever in connection with its use.

For Whom Is This Book Intended? This book is intended for entrepreneurs, business owners, investors, and anyone who is playing the long game in their professional and financial pursuits. It's for those who understand that success is not achieved overnight but through consistent effort, strategic planning, and a commitment to staying engaged in their endeavors. Whether you are managing real estate investments, running a business, or building a diversified portfolio, the principles outlined here are designed to guide you toward sustainable growth and resilience.

What People Are Saying...

Introspective, Thought Provoking, And Kind

"What is a Boaz? Yes, that was my first thought. I wasn't sure if what I was about to read was a religious book or a business book. Turns out it's both. And the further I read, the more I saw where Jeff's heart was. Wow, it's introspective, thought provoking and kind. Oh and I love the interviews." – **Brad Simmons**, Marketing Director, Bluegrass Team www.BlueGrassTeam.com

What A Great Book

"I am so proud of you! What a great book, beautiful concept, well written and thought out. Really liked the interviews. Please introduce me to Kira, she seems like an amazing woman of God. Thank you for allowing me to read this, it's really good!" – **Wendy Sweet,** Carolina Hard Money www.CarolinaHardMoney.com

Chock-full Of Timeless, Real-World Advice

"Boaz on Business is absolutely chock-full of timeless, real-world advice on how to build generational wealth instead of just getting by day to day, as far-too-many business owners do. Its subtitle states that its wisdom applies "during chaotic times" -- but it should be clear to even the most casual observer that we will very likely be living in chaotic times from now well into the future. Therefore, this masterpiece should be read and studied now, and then referred to over and over throughout the reader's lifetime."
– **Steve Sipress**, Founder of The WOW! Strategy™

Serves As A Powerful Guide

"The Bible is rich with examples of remarkable leaders, and Jeff Watson has expertly highlighted one often overlooked: Boaz. Through the narrative of the book of Ruth, Jeff unpacks timeless business and leadership principles that resonate in any era. Boaz's life exemplifies success not only in business but also in character, and this book serves as a powerful guide to help you achieve that same balance in your own life."
– **Jordan Baker**, www.BakerConstructionCo.com

Amazingly Written, Theologically Accurate.

"This is the most insightful and inspiring books I have read about wealth and generosity. It is amazingly written, theologically accurate and business savvy." – **Tom Melzoni**, Senior Vice President, Horizons Stewardship, www.Horizons.net

This Book Challenges Readers

"Boaz on Business by Jeff Watson is a masterful blend of Biblical wisdom and practical business insights. Drawing from the timeless story of Boaz in the book of Ruth, Jeff unpacks principles of integrity, generosity, legacy and leadership that resonate powerfully in today's business & investing marketplace. With compelling insights and actionable advice, this book challenges readers to build businesses rooted in purpose and character. Whether you're a seasoned entrepreneur or just starting out, Boaz on Business offers transformative lessons for success. A must-read for those who value faith and strategy!" – **Jim Ingersoll,** Founder, Elite Deal Maker, www.EliteDealMakers.com

I Will Be Giving A Copy To Every New Mentor

"Every beginner to seasoned entrepreneur will enhance their business performance and focus their mindset on HOW to run a long lasting, SATISFYING business adopting the principles, concepts and discussions in this book. I will be giving a copy to every new entrepreneur I mentor, as well as my own children. What could be more important than biblically backed guidance on running a healthy business with wealth that sustains generations of both men and women." – **Jennifer Steward**

This Is Going To Serve So Many

"In Boaz on Business Jeff Watson marries perfectly 30-years of business wisdom through the lens of Biblical truth. The way each principle starts in the scripture and ends with practical business application makes it so digestible; The CLEAR acronym is also particularly powerful. This is going to serve so many and is already blessing me." – **Brian Lawrence,** Founder, Winsight, www.WinsightCo.com

Table of Contents

The Long Game

"Success in business and investing is not about quick wins; it's about the long game. Like Boaz, who stayed present and involved through the ups and downs of his harvest season, successful investors and business owners know that being strategically involved over time is what builds lasting wealth and legacy. Playing the long game means being prepared, staying vigilant, and making thoughtful decisions that align with your values and goals. This mindset allows you to navigate challenges, capitalize on opportunities, and build a future that extends beyond immediate gains."

– Jeff Watson

Foreword
Rob Anspach

When Jeff Watson first reached out to me about this book, *Boaz on Business*, we had three long phone calls. Each one was a deep dive into Jeff's mission, his vision for this book, and what he truly wanted to accomplish. Jeff wasn't looking for a quick "yes man" approach. He needed to make sure I understood the significance behind what he was creating, and more importantly, who this book was for. He was determined that I had a real sense of who the readers would be—the entrepreneurs, investors, and legacy builders—and how the lessons of Boaz could serve them in such a chaotic world.

Those calls were about more than business or book production; they were about getting on the same page with Jeff's mission. He made it clear that this book wasn't just another title on a shelf; it was meant to make an impact. Jeff wanted the principles in *Boaz on Business* to be a guide for those navigating challenging economic times, showing them how to build multi-generational wealth while staying true to their values. And honestly, the more we talked, the more I felt this was a book I had to be part of.

It's a rare privilege when you get the opportunity to work on something that not only inspires you but also aligns so closely with the values you live by. That's how I felt with *Boaz on Business*. Jeff and I, we've both seen entrepreneurs come and go. We know that business isn't just about making money—it's about creating something lasting, something that endures beyond the ups and downs of any market cycle. Boaz, as Jeff points out, is the ultimate example of that. He built wealth, but more importantly, he built legacy.

Working on this book wasn't just a job for me; it was an honor. Jeff, with his passion and insight, has taken a story that many might know as a Biblical love story and transformed it into a blueprint for business owners and investors. And let me tell you, this isn't your typical business book. It's not full of buzzwords or the latest trends. It's rooted in time-tested principles that have survived centuries—principles of generosity, risk management, integrity, and building a foundation that can withstand any storm.

I could see Jeff's heart in every conversation. He wanted to ensure that the readers would walk away from this book not just with knowledge but with actionable insights. I'm proud of what we've accomplished here together. This book is more than a compilation of ideas; it's a guidebook for those who want to build wealth and leave a meaningful legacy while doing it.

It's been a privilege to collaborate with Jeff on *Boaz on Business*. If you're reading this, you're in for a journey—one that will challenge you, inspire you, and ultimately equip you to build something that lasts.

—Rob Anspach,
Anspach Media

Introduction
Jeff Watson

Most people who are familiar with the Book of Ruth in the Bible think of it as a love story in which an older man meets a younger lady, they fall in love and get married, and they live happily ever after. Their great, great grandchild, David, goes on to accomplish great things. For the romantic, it makes for a great love story; but there is another aspect to it.

This book is inspired by my study of the Book of Ruth and what I see as a blueprint contained in it for how to run a business during chaotic times like today and how to become a mighty person of wealth. Let's look at what Boaz can teach us about how to operate a successful business and build wealth during uncertain times.

The events in the Book of Ruth in the Old Testament took place during the time when the Israelites were occupying the Promised Land. There was no consistent, centralized form of government. They did not yet have a king but were instead ruled by various judges who came and went as the need for deliverance from their enemies dictated. This period in Israel's history was characterized by enemy invasions, marauding bands of outsiders looting and stealing from them, and famines which led to population relocation.

It was also a time of religious confusion and moral decay. The Bible describes it as being a time when everyone was doing that which was right in his own eyes. Corruption and immorality had even found their way into the lives of Israel's priests, the very ones whose job it was to lead the people according to God's laws (see I Samuel 2-4 about Eli the priest and his sons). For those who want to understand better the total depravity and moral confusion of the time, read the book of Judges and see some of the horrible cultural things that were going on during this time.

All of this presented great challenges to those trying to survive in a predominantly agrarian society. Farmers and business owners back then were certainly not as geographically or technologically nimble as those of today.

In our country at present, we are seeing things that are very similar to what Boaz experienced eons ago. Whether we call it "woke" or "politically correct", people are doing what they think is right in their own eyes. There are frequent reports of religious leaders with moral failings. The news is filled with accounts regarding corruption, influence peddling, and bribery among the highest political offices in the land. Supply chain issues and food shortages are making themselves felt, and economic uncertainty is on the minds of everyone.

During turbulent times like these, it's important to remember that opportunity often occurs in the middle of chaos. Those who recognize that and take action while others are frozen with fear or doubt are the ones who will be able to create opportunities for themselves out of that chaos.

Merely recognizing that fact, however, is not enough. How can you make the most of these opportunities? What business skills are needed? What are the things required on a daily, consistent basis to achieve that success born from chaos?

It's my hope that this book will set forth in a clear and understandable way the essential principles Boaz successfully demonstrated over 2,800 years ago, during a time of great chaos, which allowed him to build success that has lasted and impacted the world and civilization for thousands of years. These principles still apply today.

Jeffery S. Watson

"Creating the right culture in your business will help ensure a strong, unified team working toward a shared vision."

You will be asked many times throughout this book, ***"How can I apply this to my business?"***

My goal is that you reflect on that question as you read each chapter. And if you can do that, you'll start to model Boaz and become more successful in business.

Now you might be asking yourself, who was Boaz?

Boaz was a man of prayer who diligently studied the Jewish law and lived in accordance with its teachings, demonstrating integrity, generosity, and reverence for God in all his actions.

In the Beginning…

"Now it came to pass in the days when the judges ruled, that there was a famine in the land." In the city of Bethlehem, Elimelech and his family were feeling its effects. The time had come to tell his wife Naomi and their two sons, Mahlon and Chilion, of his decision. They were selling their land, quitting farming, and leaving for Moab on the other side of the Dead Sea where the famine hadn't reached. Elimelech couldn't tell them how long they would be there, but since they were leaving to "sojourn" in Moab, he probably had plans to return to Bethlehem after their temporary stay.

"And Elimelech, Naomi's husband, died; and she was left, and her two sons." At some point after the family had arrived in Moab, Naomi found herself alone with her two boys in a strange land, facing the challenge of starting a new life as a widow. A great blessing for her, however, was that she had two sons to take on the responsibility of caring for her. They each married a Moabite woman, one named Orpah and the other named Ruth, and Naomi and her sons settled into their new lives in Moab.

"And Mahlon and Chilion died also both of them; and the woman was left of her two sons and her husband." Naomi had left her homeland, she lost her husband, and now her sons were gone. It was more than she could bear. She couldn't bring back Elimelech or her boys, but there was one thing she could go back to – Bethlehem. She had heard that the famine was over and there was bread in the land.

The day arrived, and Naomi set out on her journey accompanied by her daughters-in law. As they left their house in Moab behind them, Naomi realized that while she was heading to her home, Orpah and Ruth were leaving theirs. She pleaded with the women to go back and make lives for themselves in Moab. Even if it were possible for Naomi to have two more sons, surely the women

13

wouldn't want to wait for years for them to grow up so they could marry a brother of their deceased husbands, as was the custom.

With tearful goodbyes, the women made their decisions. Orpah turned around and retraced her steps, but Ruth vowed that she would not leave Naomi. "For whither thou goest, I will go; and where thou lodgest, I will lodge: thy people shall be my people, and thy God my God."

Naomi and Ruth headed in the direction that would take them to Bethlehem. It had been ten years since she left. It was time for Naomi to go home.

Chapter 1: The Man

"A mighty man of wealth."

Boaz is introduced in Ruth 2 as being "a mighty man of wealth" who was "of the family of Elimelech". We know nothing of his upbringing or immediate family, but by reading between the lines, we can gain insight into what his early life might have been like.

Later in the story, we will read that Boaz went to the gate of the city and sat down when it came time to do some important business. As a young man, Boaz probably sat near the gate of the city of Bethlehem and watched men do business, learning their strategies and negotiation techniques. He listened carefully as landowners and farmers discussed how they ran their operations. This was the place where Boaz began making his networking connections.

Boaz also paid careful attention in the synagogue listening to the reading of the scrolls and studying the law. He learned many principles from the laws God gave His people that governed their lives, and he understood how to apply the principles he learned to his business.

Since nothing is mentioned to suggest otherwise, we can assume that Boaz was unmarried. Maybe he had married, but his wife died in childbirth, leaving him a childless widower who was able to have empathy for those who found themselves in that same situation.

There is no indication that Boaz was an old, lonely, bitter, selfish man. In fact, he appears to be the exact opposite of an Ebenezer Scrooge.

The actions and attitudes that Boaz demonstrated suggest that he was a powerful and authoritative force in his community and commanded great respect. He had a positive, helpful, outgoing personality and was not stingy with his time or resources. Rather, he was known for being both wealthy and generous.

What we do know about Boaz is that he was a farmer/business owner/real estate investor who, at the very least, had significant land which included fields of barley and wheat, and he would have had the livestock necessary to take care of that land. He is seen as a reverent steward of the resources with which God had blessed him. We are introduced to him as he arrived in his fields at the start of the barley harvest and greeted the reapers.

"The Lord be with you. And they answered him, The Lord bless thee." From this initial exchange, we learn something else about Boaz. His faith in God was an evident and vital part of his life. He recognized that even as the owner of his own business and as one known to be a mighty man of wealth, he was accountable to a higher spiritual authority, and he had to answer to God for how he managed the resources with which he had been blessed.

How can I apply this to my business?

1. Learn and develop necessary business skills.
We live in a time when we have unparalleled opportunities to connect with likeminded people, both physically and virtually, so we can grow and educate ourselves. In the world of business, we often hear two things: (1) you rarely want to be the smartest person in the room when you are seeking to learn, and (2) you will become like the five people you hang out with the most. In fact, there are multiple organizations that exist solely for the purpose of developing networking opportunities so that people from different industries and backgrounds can come together to share resources with one another.

It is sad, but true, that most educational institutions in America are designed to produce highly skilled and well-trained *workers* in various industries. Even trade schools teach people how to *work* in businesses rather than how to *start and run* their own businesses.

In response, various information marketers have created online academies, boot camps, etc., to teach people how to become entrepreneurs in specific areas of the economy. Some are worthwhile, but some end up being nothing more than shiny-object, profit-making opportunities for the promoters.

I have found that the most effective form of entrepreneurial education can be found in what are known as "masterminds". Business owners and operators from different sectors of an industry and geographic locations come together to share with each other the problems, challenges, and opportunities in their respective businesses, and they receive feedback from others who may have been there, done that, and figured it out.

Not all masterminds are created equal, however. Some, unfortunately, are populated by people who show up to take, take, take but do very little giving or sharing. Others are operated by people who see them as their own profit centers and design them to attract as many people as possible instead of thinking of the quality of the relationships and networking that need to be developed.

It's important to spend time with those who are at a higher level than you in your specific industry or profession. It's like playing chess with grand masters to improve your own chess playing. Networking groups, masterminds, conferences, and seminars can be productive ways to grow your knowledge base and learn new skills for your business. I would caution you, however, with this analogy: when eating fish, enjoy the meal, but make sure you avoid the bones. The power of these groups is also known to the unscrupulous and con artists who frequently troll these areas looking for new victims.

I'm reminded of what it says in Psalm 1:1 (which, as it happens, was most likely written by David, the great-grandson of Boaz): "Blessed is the man that walketh not in the counsel of the ungodly, nor standeth in the way of sinners, nor sitteth in the seat of the scornful."

For the business owner, I would flip it around and paraphrase it this way: "Blessed is the business owner who walks in the counsel of Godly men, associates with the wise and the righteous, and sits at the table of the grateful and humble."

Applying this passage of Scripture to us today, I suggest you avoid having close associations with those whose moral and philosophical perspectives do not align with yours. Filter and process all new information you receive to see if it is congruent with or properly challenges your established value system.

An important concept for all entrepreneurs to understand is that your network becomes your net worth. Having the right mindset when approaching any type of networking or educational gathering is crucial. Ask yourself what you have to offer and how you can use that to help others who can in turn help you.

One of the biggest turnoffs when sitting in mastermind meetings is encountering someone with an entitlement mentality. They believe if they merely ask, someone in the room is going to solve all their problems or give them substantial resources or knowledge in exchange for nothing.

One of the fundamental rules of true, ethical, moral capitalism is that a capitalist should always give as good as or better than what they receive.

In an exchange between two such capitalists, each is giving up something of value to get something they want even more. That mindset is essential for developing as a business owner and getting the maximum benefit from the meetings and conferences you attend to acquire new skills for your profession or business.

2. Recognize your accountability to God.

Whether you are born into a family with wealth, or you are a first-generation, aspiring millionaire, it's important to remember that you didn't acquire your wealth on your own. An important aspect of our attitude toward what we have is borne out in studies and observations that others have made as well.

There is a high correlation between financial success and a faith in God that is a vital, deep-rooted part of one's life. This is pointed out in books written by Rabbi Daniel Lapin and in books about millionaires written by the late Dr. Thomas Stanley.

Those who have looked deeper into this correlation have found a common characteristic among the wealthy they studied: a true, vital faith in God which results in ultra-high integrity.

Becoming a mighty person of wealth involves recognizing that you are accountable not only to those who work with you and for you, but more importantly, to God Himself, which will bring into your heart and mind the high level of integrity needed to be truly successful on all levels.

Applying Boaz to Investing:
The Eddie Speed Interview

Jeff Watson: I'm here with my good friend, Eddie Speed. Eddie, you and I have been through a lot, seen a lot, and I know there's plenty more ahead for us. Let's dive into something we both know well—legacy. Specifically, passing a business on to the next generation and getting them involved. We're both navigating through some pretty chaotic times, so I'd love to hear your thoughts on this.

Eddie Speed: Absolutely, Jeff.

Jeff Watson: What's on your heart and mind when you think about the business you've built? What advice would you give to people who don't have the decades of experience you do—or the influence of an amazing father-in-law like you had? How do they transition a business to the next generation

Eddie Speed: First off, I was really fortunate to have my father-in-law. He was always thinking 20 years ahead, which shaped the way I look at things. He had a wealth mentality, and that mindset stuck with me from the time I met him at 20 years old.
Jeff Watson: Hold on, Eddie—when you say he was always thinking 20 years ahead, what exactly do you mean?

Eddie Speed: He was constantly focused on the long game. He wasn't just looking at the short-term returns on his investments; he was laser-focused on the long-term impact. What would this decision mean 20 years from now?

Jeff Watson: Got it. And you mentioned he was a wealth investor. How does that tie in with this long-term outlook?

Eddie Speed: Let me give you some context, Jeff. Over the last dozen years, I've been around the biggest house buyers in the country, and we've been in those masterminds together, right? You've seen it too.

Jeff Watson: Yeah, I know exactly what you mean.

Eddie Speed: These guys have seen cycles where they've made more money in a single year than they could've ever dreamed of back in high school. They weren't Harvard grads—most were like me, just figuring it out along the way. But here's the key thing my father-in-law taught me early on: "If your net worth isn't growing faster than your income, you're going in the wrong direction."

Jeff Watson: Wow, Eddie, that's profound. Can you repeat that?

Eddie Speed: He always said, "If your net worth isn't growing faster than your income…" In other words, you might be earning more, but if you're spending it all and not building your net worth, you're missing the mark.

Jeff Watson: That's a game-changer. So, it's about focusing on net worth once your income is stable, rather than blowing money on things that don't build wealth.

Eddie Speed: Exactly. You've got to be disciplined about directing your income toward building wealth, rather than just spending it. My father-in-law drilled that into me from day one. And as you know, Jeff, he passed away at just 59 years old. But even 27 years later, his widow has lived a very comfortable life, thanks to the foundation he set.

Jeff Watson: That speaks volumes about legacy, Eddie. His vision has truly carried forward.

Eddie Speed: That's right. We've followed both his wishes and hers. We've been managing the family business alongside the other businesses I've been running. But the family business, which revolves around investing in notes, is a lot less labor-intensive than managing rental properties. We don't have to deal with the headache of overseeing a thousand rental units.

Jeff Watson: Let's pause right there. I want you to say that again—it takes less work to own notes than…

Eddie Speed: ...than it does to manage rental properties.

Jeff Watson: Exactly.

Eddie Speed: To put it simply, we could manage a thousand notes with a fraction of the effort—about 1/10th of the labor compared to managing a thousand rentals.

Jeff Watson: 1/10th of the labor, 1/10th of the management costs, 1/10th of the overhead, 1/10th of the stress—1/10th of everything.

Eddie Speed: Exactly. Now, my father-in-law originally made his wealth from rental properties—he owned trailer parks, houses, multifamily units, you name it. But he eventually realized that notes were an incredible wealth-building tool because they didn't need constant attention to generate returns.

Jeff Watson: Yeah.

Eddie Speed: And you know I got into the business too. I used my position on Main Street to find notes that I didn't flip—I kept them. That's how I built wealth. Now, here's where the family dynamic comes in. Martha's done very well with our retirement model of buying notes, especially by recapitalizing some of our funds by selling off the front payments on note partials.

Jeff Watson: Right, right.

Eddie Speed: But now Martha is at a point in her life where she doesn't want to deal with the day-to-day grind anymore.

Jeff Watson: She wants those grandbabies in her arms—that's what she wants!

Eddie Speed: Exactly. We've implemented this wealth-building strategy not just for her mother's retirement, but for us, our kids, and now even our grandkids. But here's the thing, Jeff—my kids don't want to grind in the note business every day.

Jeff Watson: Okay.

Eddie Speed: For example, my daughter is a professional ballet dancer.

Jeff Watson: Yep.

Eddie Speed: She likes notes, but her real passion is ballet.

Jeff Watson: But Eddie, her love for ballet combined with what she's learned from you and Martha is now helping her build a business in the ballet world.

Eddie Speed: That's absolutely true. You know her well.

Jeff Watson: I do. I even helped her with something just in the last 24 hours. She might not be a note investor like you, but she's definitely an entrepreneur.

Eddie Speed: And that's perfectly fine. The influence we've had on her has given her a business mindset that's quite uncommon in the ballet world.

Jeff Watson: I'd say it's more than a little uncommon, Eddie.

Eddie Speed: I don't want to offend the ballet industry by suggesting she's the only one with business savvy, but she's far more business-minded than most of the people she's encountered in her field. The point is, Jeff, my kids, like my students, want notes as an investment strategy—but they don't want to build an entire note business.

Jeff Watson: Right. They've figured out what your father-in-law taught you. They're using the same technique to build wealth, looking decades ahead.

Eddie Speed: Exactly. But there's a balance, Jeff—wealth needs to be weighed against the effort it takes to manage it.

Jeff Watson: Absolutely.

Eddie Speed: I'm going to poke a bit at our real estate-centric friends. While I do like property, I'm far more focused on notes. A lot of people are building their wealth through businesses that they assume their kids will love as much as they do. But I think many of them are going to be in for a surprise.

Jeff Watson: Eddie, I've already heard the same thing from all five of my kids. They don't want the houses, they don't want the buildings—they want the checks that show up regularly. What they're telling me is similar to what your kids are telling you: they want cash flow from notes, they want cash flow from investments, but they don't want the day-to-day heavy lifting.

Eddie Speed: Exactly. It's not that they aren't talented at what they do—they are. But you and I have a deep passion for the business, and that kind of love for it isn't necessarily transferable.

Jeff Watson: Exactly. Now, I want to circle back to something you mentioned earlier. Over the past dozen years, you've been around people who, in some years, made more money than they ever imagined possible. But what about your mindset compared to theirs? What sets you apart?

Eddie Speed: Well, my advantage is that I've been in this game for decades. I've seen the good times and the bad times. I've lived through more market cycles than most of them have.

Jeff Watson: Let's talk about those bad times, Eddie. In the book of Ruth, we see that Boaz came out of a rough period as a mighty man of wealth. How do you see opportunity during tough times?

Eddie Speed: Whenever the market turns bad, there's always tremendous opportunity—if you take the right actions, often contrary to what others are doing.

Jeff Watson: I want you to say that again, because that's profound. And then, explain what you mean by it.

Eddie Speed: In any disruptive market, there are specific moves you can make—usually the opposite of what everyone else is doing—that put you in a position to gain while they're losing.

Jeff Watson: So, it's like drinking upstream from the herd. While they're zigging, you're zagging.

Eddie Speed: Exactly. Like Warren Buffett said, "When people are greedy, be scared. When people are scared, be greedy." Now, don't take that literally as being greedy—it's about being opportunistic.

Jeff Watson: Opportunistic, yes. So, let's shift back to legacy. You've absorbed what your father-in-law taught you, you've built on it, and you see how it's benefiting your family. You've got this across four generations now—what other pearls of wisdom do you have when it comes to a legacy mindset?

Eddie Speed: Well, future generations will need enough knowledge to make smart decisions at an executive level. They don't have to know everything, but they need the basics—the "ESPN version," so to speak.

Jeff Watson: I like that.

Eddie Speed: We had to play the games to learn what happens in real time. But future generations can get the play-by-play, and that knowledge can become part of the legacy. You can even put it in writing for them, just like my father-in-law did. He essentially added a codicil to his will with a letter. You know what the first line said?

Jeff Watson: I'd love to hear it.

Eddie Speed: "Money spent on fond memories is never wasted."

Jeff Watson: Wow. That's powerful.

Eddie Speed: Now, my father-in-law wasn't the type to brag about spending money, so for him to say that—it's a real gem. The point is, don't be so focused on being economical that you forget to enjoy life.

Jeff Watson: Exactly.

Eddie Speed: For someone thinking about legacy—while they're still alive—maybe one or two of their kids can step into more of a management role in the business.

Jeff Watson: Yes, while you're still around to guide them.

Eddie Speed: Exactly. You need to lay out the strategy for them— again, even if it's just the "ESPN version"—and make sure they have a clear risk management profile. It doesn't have to be complicated, but it needs to be clear.

Jeff Watson: It absolutely has to be clear. I had one of these legacy conversations with my middle daughter. To sum it up, she said,

"Dad, teach us what we need to know, and don't try to control everything once you're gone."

Eddie Speed: That's a great point.

Jeff Watson: Hearing that from one of your kids hits differently than from a colleague or mentor. When my daughter said, "Teach us what we need to know, but don't try to control things after you're gone," it really stuck with me. I don't know about you, Eddie, but I can be a bit of a control freak.

Eddie Speed: Oh, trust me, Jeff—I know. My father-in-law would've been the same way. He died unexpectedly, but if he'd known, I guarantee he would've made sure we had everything we needed to know. What he left behind essentially said, "I've taught you good judgment—now go use it."

Jeff Watson: That's a powerful legacy principle right there. "I've taught you good judgment—go use good judgment."

Chapter 2: His Wealth

"Boaz displayed generosity in sharing his wealth."

Common sense tells us you aren't born with the knowledge it takes to be a person of wealth. Even if you do inherit wealth, it can be easily squandered by the time you are a mature adult if you don't know what to do, particularly during times of economic and political uncertainty. So, how did Boaz become a mighty man of wealth?

First, we need to remember the background of this story. There had been a severe famine in the land, one which had sent Elimelech and his family and many others to live in places where they could find food and survive. While many had sold their land and moved away, Boaz stayed put. He continued to grow crops as best he could.

Boaz was a member of the tribe of Judah, which controlled that part of Israel at the time. Boaz probably inherited his lands and property from his father, who had inherited it from his father, and so on, going back a couple hundred years. A person's wealth was based primarily on how much land they owned, how much livestock they had, and the yield from their crops.

Given that Boaz had survived the famine, it's a reasonable assumption that he knew how to maintain his wealth through difficult times with diligence and hard work. Since he may not have been married or had any children, Boaz would have had more time to devote to his business and work endeavors.

Boaz may have had adequate reserves that allowed him to buy land when others were having to sell. This land would yield a return and provide a source of income. He diversified those assets by planting different crops so he could allocate his labor resources based on the time of the harvest for each crop. He chose barley and wheat which had multiple uses such as feeding both people and animals and even making beverages, thus giving him a greater market for his products.

It's worth noting that during this time in Israel's history, various judges ruled the land, and there was a lot of oppression from outside countries against Israel. Not only did Boaz demonstrate the ability to keep and grow his wealth through a famine, but he did it during a time of political uncertainty and invasions or attacks from other nations.

Thomas Manton, an English Puritan clergyman, wrote, "God gave us wealth, not that we should be hoarders but dispensers." When we look at the actions of Boaz, we see someone who understood this principle. Boaz displayed generosity in sharing his wealth. In case you are not familiar with the story, let me give you some additional background.

When Naomi and Ruth arrived in Bethlehem, they found themselves in an unenviable situation. As widows with no sons to provide for them, things would have been very difficult. In the Law that God gave the Israelites, farmers were given specific instructions regarding the harvesting of their crops. They were not to harvest all the way to the corners of the fields, and they were not to go back and do a second harvest. If some of the grain or produce fell to the ground, it was to be left there. Those who were poor or who were resident foreigners in their land were then allowed to go through the fields and gather what they could. Widows and orphans especially were included in the group of those who were allowed to come and glean in the fields.

Ruth took on the task of finding a field where they would allow her to enter and gather grain, and she "just happened" to come to part of a field that belonged to Boaz, who "just happened" to be a relative of her late father-in-law. On that day, Boaz came to the field to see how things were progressing with the harvest, and his attention was drawn to the new woman who had come to glean. She was different from the others who were gleaning. Upon learning from his overseer who Ruth was, Boaz began giving instructions that would allow his generosity to go above and beyond the minimum of what God had commanded.

31

As an example of his generosity, Boaz instructed his overseer and the young men who worked for him to watch over Ruth and make sure no one bothered her. He then called Ruth to him and let her know that he had heard about all she had done for her mother-in-law. Boaz instructed Ruth to stay in his fields and not go to any other fields to glean. He told her to stay by the young women who worked for him and follow them in the field. She was also invited to spend her mealtime with his reapers and with Boaz himself, sharing the food and water that he provided for them.

Boaz could have looked at Ruth as just another poor person, and a foreigner at that, and been content to allow her to work as every other gleaner in his fields, but something about her and her story made him go the extra mile with his generosity. His workers were not only informed that Ruth was to share in the meals, but they were to purposely drop some of the grain on the ground so she could gather more.

At the end of Ruth's first day of gleaning in the fields of Boaz, she beat out what she had gathered and found she had the equivalent of about a bushel of barley. Because of the generosity of Boaz, Ruth had more than she needed and was able to share the abundance of her gleaning and part of her gifted lunch with Naomi.

It's doubtful that Boaz's encounter with Ruth was the first time he had shown extra generosity to someone in need. His actions demonstrated his understanding that wealth was not something to be hoarded. It was to be shared with others, not just for the benefit of the recipients, but for his benefit and blessing as well.

How can I apply this to my business?

I'm sure you'll agree that at the time of the writing of this book, we are living in a time of economic uncertainty. There is great division in our country when it comes to social, political, and cultural policies and changes. We are watching the demise of China and rise of India on the world stage, and we are seeing the United

States become much more nationalistic and far less global in our trade and foreign policy. All of this has an impact on entrepreneurs and business owners.

We are also dealing with the current realities of high inflation, labor shortages, supply chain shortages and delays, and rising costs for insurance and taxes. The question then becomes how one maintains, or even grows, wealth during such times of uncertainty. There are some things we can derive from Boaz and his ancestors.

1. Invest in tangible assets that consistently produce income.

Purchase quality, cash-flowing assets whose values are strong and have room to grow over the long term. By "quality" real estate, I mean something that consistently produces income such as rent or cash crops. In the eyes of the world, one of the most important pieces of real estate one can own is American farmland given the geographic and topographic benefits we have in this country. Whether we own farmland or apartment complexes or single-family houses, we are looking for things that consistently produce income. Assets that produce cash flow are desirable since they will help cover the cost of your liabilities.

Maximize the income being produced by raising rents or prices where you can while you can. Make sure your investments pay monthly cash flow that is above what you need to live on.

2. Understand the importance of reserves and diversification.

We know that during the time of Boaz, there was a lot of political and economic uncertainty in Israel; but we also know that at a key business opportunity, Boaz had sufficient liquidity to buy back (redeem) the land that Naomi and her late husband had sold (more on that later).

During times of uncertainty today, there will be business owners who, for a host of reasons, need to liquidate assets at fire-sale prices. By having cash reserves, you can seize those opportunities. An uncomfortable, but popular, statement is that the best time to buy real estate is when there is blood in the streets, including when some of that blood is your own.

Having ample reserves available isn't important just for being able to take advantage of opportunities when they come.

The unexpected *will* happen.

Prioritize saving diligently until you have a minimum of 3 months of living expenses and 3 months of business expenses. To help you do that, evaluate your personal and business budgets to remove or lower the amounts spent on discretionary items. "Lifestyle creep" (the tendency to increase spending as income increases but without saving or paying down debt) can happen slowly and unintentionally, and it leads to financial setbacks and has long-term consequences for retirement.

The other key element to help you thrive in uncertain times is diversity. You need to have assets in multiple sectors and only allow a small portion to be invested in things that have high risk and the accompanying high reward. Solomon, the great-great grandson of Boaz, advised that you divide your assets eight different ways because you do not know what may happen. I call this the "pizza pie principle" since pizzas are typically cut into eight slices. Here are my recommendations for those eight slices.

There are four categories of low- or no-load mutual funds into which I recommend people invest their money – international, growth, growth and income, and regressive growth. Having investments in each of those four categories will keep you balanced. Find funds that have a good, consistent track record of delivering a good rate of return over time (look at the last 10 years at least) and avoid funds that have high fees associated with them. That's one half of the pizza.

In the other half of the pizza, two slices can focus on owning residential real estate. While there are a multitude of books, TV shows, YouTube channels, podcasts and more devoted to investing in real estate, there are two fundamental rules: 1) Keep it simple, and 2) only invest in what you know and understand. Being a housing provider isn't necessarily for everyone. If you decide to make residential real estate part of your portfolio, make sure you get good education on the subject, and that doesn't mean having to pay for expensive coaching programs pitched by famous people on TV or the internet. Learning how to manage real estate is a skill that can pay you significant profits over time. As you age and the "thrill" of management fades, you can move away from single-family residential properties and move more towards investing as a limited partner in large, multi-family syndications. That way, you will get the benefits of owning residential real estate while escaping the headaches that come with it.

Another slice can include some form of commercial real estate, being very careful to pay attention to demographic trends. For example, those who were watching could see that a trend against commercial office space was beginning even before 2020. That trend was accelerated by Covid as well as changing environmental and social factors.

The final slice of the pizza can be used to own good, performing, secured debt for which you, the investor, are collecting consistent monthly payments as if you were a bank. Those investments can often be structured in such a way as to beat the interest rate on bonds, certificates of deposit, and other fixed-rate investments.

For those of you who find these recommendations a bit too aggressive for your comfort level, you can certainly look at allocating your investments differently. I recommend avoiding single stocks, however. I also suggest you have a portion of your overall investment in cash so you can maintain liquidity and take advantage of investment opportunities when they arise.

However, you choose to allocate your investments, always invest in assets you control and understand rather than spreading them thinly across unfamiliar markets. Only a limited amount of your investment portfolio (basically money that you would be just as willing to light on fire!) should be in things with high risk, and these investments should be avoided completely if you don't understand them. These investments include things like most cryptocurrency, NFTs, penny stocks, Forex, and day trading.

3. Be generous with your wealth.

One of the leading examples of a business today that practices what we see Boaz demonstrating is Chick-fil-A...OK, those of you who know me well, I can hear you laughing at how I managed to work in my favorite source of sustenance! Upon visiting a well-run Chick-fil-A operation, which I may have just a bit of experience doing (you're laughing at me again!), you will see that the local Chick-fil-A franchise is involved in community activities. Even those working on the front lines taking orders at the registers are given some discretion over how to bless customers with free food or drink items.

On a Sunday afternoon in December 2017, there was a massive power outage at the Hartsfield-Jackson Airport in Atlanta, Georgia. Thousands of stranded passengers were shuttled to the Georgia International Convention Center to shelter for the night. If you understand the culture of Chick-fil-A, which is headquartered in Atlanta, you know that they do not open for business on Sunday, but that didn't prevent them from helping others in need that day. The CEO of Chick-fil-A, Dan Cathy, mobilized the operators of some of his restaurants in that city, and he was right beside his workers helping to hand out the 5,302 chicken sandwiches that were donated to hungry travelers.

We may not be part of a famous, well-run chicken business, or any other multi-billion-dollar company with franchises for that matter, but we all can make sure our businesses do things to help others and show generosity. Are we offering discounted prices to "widows and orphans", a term used in the Bible to represent those who are the neediest? Are we able to set aside concerns regarding taxation and just give to others, whether from our businesses or personally from our take-home pay?

The phrase "giving back" bothers me because it implies that you took something from someone. I prefer the phrase "giving from", which means I take something that I honestly earned in exchange for my time, talent, and effort, and I choose to bless someone else with it or give them the opportunity to earn for themselves at a better rate. Giving from our Spiritual well motives us to give from our earthly portfolio.

4. Avoid these things to maintain your wealth.

Any discussion on strategies for maintaining and growing wealth must include some things to avoid which can quickly deplete wealth:

- **High-risk ventures**, unless you are prepared to lose every bit of capital invested into that venture.
- **Significant debt**, as the cost of paying for that debt can quickly devour profits. This is one of the two primary reasons that cause many businesses to fail in their first three to five years.
- **Failing to accurately manage tax liabilities**, which is the other main reason for businesses failing to be successful. These include employment taxes, real estate taxes, income taxes, sales taxes, and that's just the beginning of what business owners face.
- **Failing to be properly insured**, the purpose of which is to mitigate risk that you are otherwise unable to handle. Insurance should not be used as an investment or savings vehicle. It's intended to be a means of preventing exposure to costs which might bankrupt or cause a person or business to become insolvent.

- **Failing to accurately track your numbers**, which is a must for any business owner. If you do not know your numbers, such as the cost for you to obtain a new customer, your average profit margin on a new customer, your return on ad spending for marketing campaigns, your overall cost of doing business, and your true net profit, then you are lacking the necessary information to know if you can stay in business or not. Way too many entrepreneurs focus on gross income and fail to look at the net income after all costs and taxes.

Applying Boaz to Strategy:
The Kira Golden Interview - Part 1

Jeff Watson: Jeff Watson here. I'm with my friend Kira Golden. We are going to do an interview regarding *Boaz on Business*, and Kira is going to discuss it from Ruth's perspective. So to begin, Kira, you and I have been doing business together now for a few years. We do a lot of stuff in the real estate space. Why don't you go ahead and tell us a little bit about who you are, and then let's talk about the book *Boaz on Business* I'm writing, and what you see from Ruth's perspective?

Kira Golden: Thanks, Jeff. So, you know, it's funny. Over the years, I think one of the biggest realizations for me—maybe something Ruth would have felt too—is that I'm not entirely sure who I am. I used to define myself by a long list of roles: I'm a mom, I have two kids, I run businesses. But more and more, I've come to see myself less as someone who needs to be validated and more as someone who's simply being used by God. It's less about me and more about what He's doing through me. So, if I'm being honest, I don't think my identity matters as much as the work He has for me. I'm just a conduit.

Jeff Watson: One of those identities, though, would be in the business arena, and another in the real estate space, right?

Kira Golden: Yeah, definitely. And when I think about the business space and real estate, it ties back to Ruth in a really interesting way. Ruth found herself without a husband, and suddenly, it's on her to provide. She had to step up, not because it was the ideal scenario but because it was necessary. She had to do it humbly. It wasn't a glamorous "boss babe" situation like we see today—there's this whole perception that women in business need to be powerhouses, right? But for me, and I think for Ruth too, it wasn't about power or ambition. It was about duty. For a long time, I tried to project this image that wasn't really true to what was driving me. I didn't want people to know I was just doing what needed to be done. There was no hunger for dominance—it was more about being faithful to the path in front of me.

Jeff Watson: So I like where you picked up with Ruth, but I want to step back to one of her earlier decisions. Ruth made the decision to trust God. She said to Naomi, "Where you go, I go; your people will be my people, and your God my God." That choice led her to the point where she had to care for Naomi, and then she had to go to work to do it.

Kira Golden: Exactly. And I think that speaks to something we see later in scripture. It took me a while to fully understand, but Jesus says things like, "You'll hate your mother and father, you'll hate your own life to love me." For a long time, I thought that seemed kind of harsh—why would a God of love ask that of us? But over time, I've come to see it differently. It's not about hating people— it's about rejecting anything that isn't aligned with God's plan. Ruth does that when she leaves her people, her culture, and her gods behind. She could've stayed, remarried, had a comfortable life. But she didn't. She chose Naomi and God's bigger purpose, and that's something we can all learn from.

Jeff Watson: Ruth could have stuck with what she knew, but I also want to give a shout-out to Naomi. There had to be something about Naomi's faith and life that initially drew Ruth and her other daughter-in-law to her. At the crossroads, Ruth stayed with Naomi while the other daughter-in-law went home. And when Naomi and Ruth returned to Bethlehem, Naomi was pretty bitter—she even says, "Call me Bitter," because she's lost everything. But Ruth didn't let that stop her from stepping up and doing what had to be done.

Kira Golden: Yeah, and I can relate to that. I think I might've had my own "Naomi period" before entering my "Ruth period." If we're talking about women in business, here's something I've noticed. People often say things like, "Men can't handle a powerful woman." And maybe there's some truth to that sometimes, but what I've observed is that we often confuse empowerment with rage.

Jeff Watson: Or bitterness.

Kira Golden: Exactly. When we're bitter or angry, it can come off as powerful, but that's not true power. There's a big difference between Naomi's bitterness and Ruth's power. Ruth was a powerful woman, but not because she was strutting around, showing off. Her power came from a place of kindness, humility, and obedience—qualities rooted in the fruits of the Spirit. I don't think people—whether men or women—have trouble with that kind of power. It's the other kind, the one driven by bitterness or insecurity, that clashes.

Jeff Watson: I think that's a really good point. And, you know, I don't want to steal your thunder here, but Ruth is one of the few women listed in the genealogy of Jesus Christ. That says a lot about who she was, her significance, and her enduring power.

Kira Golden: Absolutely. And it's important to remember that the Bible often doesn't expand much on someone's actions—it's more about their character. Like when you asked me earlier, "Who are you?"—you didn't ask, "What do you do?" There's a difference. Ruth's story shows us the character of her heart, and from that, her actions flowed. It starts with who you are.

Jeff Watson: Let's talk about some of Ruth's actions. She decided she had to work, and she took a physically demanding, menial job—gleaning.

Kira Golden: Well, I don't think gleaning was really a "job" in the way we think of jobs today.

Jeff Watson: Oh?

41

Kira Golden: My understanding is that landowners, who were generally wealthy, were required by law not to harvest the edges of their fields. The poor could come and gather what was left. So Ruth wasn't hired by anyone—she wasn't working under someone's authority. She was humbling herself to participate in the system God designed to protect people like her. She wasn't given anything except the opportunity, and then she worked hard to make the most of it for her and Naomi.

Jeff Watson: Exactly. So the first day she goes out to glean, afterward, she realizes that God had guided her to the right field—Boaz's field. And then she does what Boaz invited her to do, and Naomi instructed her to do, which was to stick with it. Talk about that perseverance.

Kira Golden: There's a lot of humility in doing what's in front of you, especially without the security of a traditional job. Ruth wasn't just working hard—she was showing up consistently, over and over again, without anyone offering her a guarantee. She was obedient. I think the biggest takeaway for me is that she didn't give up. She had grit. She showed up, and she kept showing up.

Jeff Watson: She refused to quit. Another thing that stands out is, on her first day, she was invited to join the workers for lunch, and Boaz made sure she was well-fed. Ruth kept some of that food back and took it home to Naomi. Talk about what that reveals about her character.

Kira Golden: That shows so much about her identity in community and servant leadership. She made sure to take care of Naomi, but notice that she did eat herself. She wasn't so self-sacrificing that she ignored her own needs. There's a balance there—God blesses us so that blessings can flow *through* us, not just *to* us. Ruth understood that. She received the gift but also made sure to share it, to pass it on.

Jeff Watson: And that sharing, to me, shows how fully committed Ruth was to becoming part of Naomi's people and embracing Naomi's God. What are your thoughts on that?

Kira Golden: I think Ruth's commitment started the moment she declared it to Naomi, and it carried through. There were probably many times when she could've turned back, said, "This is too hard," and gone home. But she didn't. I see that kind of all-in commitment in business, too. As leaders, we have to ask ourselves, "Am I committed to this team, this vision?" Ruth was committed to Naomi and God's plan, no matter what came her way.

Jeff Watson: Speaking of that commitment, Ruth went back to Naomi after the first day of gleaning, and Naomi gave her advice—stick with these people. That's part of why Ruth's story has such a lasting impact.

Kira Golden: Exactly. Ruth was coachable. Naomi shows up throughout the whole story as this socially aware, emotionally intelligent figure, guiding Ruth. Ruth didn't know the customs or traditions, but she trusted Naomi's guidance. And because she was open to that mentorship, it changed the trajectory of her life—and history. Obedience, humility, and being coachable put her on the path God had prepared for her.

Jeff Watson: Yes, I completely agree. There's something really important about that discipleship from Naomi.

Kira Golden: Definitely. And I don't think it's accidental that Ruth's mentor was another woman. There's a purity in women mentoring women. Naomi understood Ruth's situation in a way that a man probably couldn't. It's not that men can't mentor women, but there's something really powerful about women guiding each other, especially in faith, business, or life. That kind of discipleship is something we need more of.

"Remember: The unexpected will happen."

Chapter 3: His Business

"Boaz understood an important aspect of operating a business – risk management."

Let's analyze the business decisions and choices Boaz made a little more closely and see what we can learn and apply to our business practices.

Business Operations

When reading chapters 2 and 3 of the Book of Ruth, it is apparent that Boaz had built a large business operation. His significant assets included real estate holdings used to grow grain and the livestock necessary to plow large fields. The fields were sizable since many reapers were needed to harvest them, and numerous gleaners could gather enough leftovers to feed their families.

As with any business, one of the biggest assets Boaz had was his human resources – the team with which he surrounded himself. Boaz's organizational structure and actions toward his overseers and reapers demonstrate his understanding of their importance to the successful operation of his business.

Boaz understood another important aspect of operating a business – risk management. He made sure his workers were taken care of with water to drink and food to eat so they could continue to be part of making his business successful, and he was right there with them through the process of getting the harvest to market.

In Ruth 3, we see a scene between Boaz and Ruth that takes place at the threshing floor. During the barley harvest, the cut stalks were transported to the threshing site which was usually on a hill so that afternoon winds would help with the winnowing process. The grain was loosed from the stalks and chaff by various methods, and it was thrown into the air to allow the wind or fans to blow away the chaff, leaving just the grain behind. This would be further sifted to remove any debris and then be put into bags to be sent to silos for storage or to markets for sale. The chaff was burned in bonfires, and the community celebrated with singing, dancing, and feasting.

We are told that following his participation in these festivities, Boaz was there at the threshing floor sleeping right next to his bags of grain, maybe out of concern over theft or loss. Through every step of the process from harvesting to threshing, Boaz was present at the times that mattered. He understood the risks to his assets and made himself part of the team helping to minimize those risks.

By being present throughout the process, he was aware of the current cultural and economic threats that his business was facing.

How can I apply this to my business?

1. Understand the value of your team.

One of the greatest assets a business owner has is their team. Boaz's approach to business emphasized the importance of understanding and valuing your team as a critical component of success. The importance of your team needs to be communicated frequently using words that are backed up by actions so that your team members feel they are a valued and essential part of the business operations.

The success of a company is due, in part, to everyone being able to come together as equals, despite having different roles and responsibilities, to get the job done.

Your team may consist of full-time and/or part-time employees, independent contractors with whom you have an ongoing relationship, and even vendors with whom you work on a regular basis. All those members of your team need to understand that they are valuable assets to your overall operation. This could mean providing adequate support, tools, or training to help them perform their jobs effectively. It definitely includes paying them what they are worth and in a timely manner.

Additionally, being involved in the day-to-day operations and having your finger on the pulse of the business rather than just overseeing from a distance allows you to understand the challenges your team faces and identify and address any risks or threats early.

When you value your team, you will be able to properly equip, train, lead, energize, and empathize with your team members.

Remember the story I shared earlier about Dan Cathy and Chick-fil-A feeding thousands because of a blackout at the Atlanta airport on a Sunday? By being present and engaged, you not only mitigate risks, but you foster a culture of trust and respect. This demonstrates value to each of your team members. They will see that you are invested in their success and the success of the business, which can increase morale and loyalty as well as productivity.

We've all been in businesses that are staffed by people who are there just to collect a paycheck. They do only what's necessary to keep from getting fired. And I'm sure we've all been in businesses where the employees are energized and enthusiastic about being there. That's because they feel they are vital members of the team. They want to make their employer successful.

Ultimately, understanding the value of your team means appreciating their unique contributions, supporting them with the necessary resources, and actively participating in processes that directly affect the business's outcomes. This approach not only safeguards your assets but also enhances the overall efficiency and resilience of your business.

2. Understand the need for risk management.
Many entrepreneurs are not good managers, let alone good at understanding risk management. To be a successful entrepreneur, you often have to take risks. This requires cat-like mental reflexes in business negotiations to distinguish between being a massively successful entrepreneur and being one who just barely gets ahead.

Occasionally, you may find an entrepreneur who does a poor job at management but is brilliant when it comes to finding deals, creating opportunities, and negotiating.

By nature, most business owners are risk takers. They want to control their own futures instead of being dependent on some other company or person with a prodigious staff, budget, and payroll that could pink slip them at any time. The perception of risk in their eyes is different from that of an ordinary person.

Risk must be categorized. Some risks are minor and may only result in temporary inconveniences or small financial setbacks if things don't go as planned. Other risks, however, may have more significant consequences and could take months or even years to overcome or could even threaten the very existence of the business.

RISK ASSESSMENT	
Level	**If you fail...**
★	...it will only cost the time and money invested into it.
★★	...it will cost more money and time than what was invested to repair the damage from failure or something not going as planned.
★★★	...there will be reputational and financial damage in addition to the loss of time and resources.
★★★★	...there will be reputational and financial damage in addition to the loss of time and resources, as well as loss of future revenue, but it's survivable with the right amount of effort and hard work.
★★★★★	...it will crush the business, bring operations to an end, and may result in bankruptcy.

When it comes to risk management, the "management" aspect is just as important as the "risk" aspect. Once an entrepreneur determines the level of risk they are facing with each operation or decision, steps can be taken to minimize and manage those risks.

Good management will reduce risks and prevent problems. It will anticipate difficulties ahead and will plan for them and have a solution ready for implementation when they come.

An important part of managing risk is to be present at critical times. I've seen business owners who put people into positions of responsibility and then thought they could "check out" from that aspect of their business, only to find later after damage had been done that the person they trusted to take care of things wasn't as skilled, disciplined, properly resourced, or trustworthy as they had thought. Had the business owner been present at important times and been checking up regularly on the various aspects of their business, problems would have been discovered much sooner, and devastating consequences could have been avoided.

Having good management means asking questions designed to get to the truth of a matter. We live in a data-driven world, but it's still important to ask questions about the data you are given. Are the numbers real? Upon what are they based? Are they just someone's theory or best guess, or is there solid evidence to support the numbers and projections?

Just as Boaz asked questions when he arrived at the barley field that day and noticed that something was different, a good risk manager must be observant and ask questions when they see that something has changed or is different from the norm in their business. A successful entrepreneur must stay on top of what is happening in every aspect of their business.

Not only do business owners reap the benefits when good risk management practices are in place, but it creates a healthier, more stable work environment in which the focus can then be on the main goal of providing goods or services that the customers want at fair prices which generate good profits. It helps eliminate the drama of operating in a pattern of having to move from one crisis situation to the next. There are times when crisis management can't be avoided – fires, floods, cyber-attacks, accidents, etc. – but good risk management will have systems and resources in place to handle those events.

Good risk management will also have business practices in place to focus on consistent, steady growth and diligent cash and resource management to help avoid the wild swings that come with taking huge risks and not being able to bear the responsibility and consequences of those risks.

At the time of this writing, we have seen interest rates tightening. Many entrepreneurs in the real estate industry have experienced significant setbacks in their businesses or have had their businesses close altogether because of their failure to properly manage risk and their business operations.

The decision to check out and be a long-distance owner who merely cashes checks and looks at a few spreadsheets will lead to a collapse of your business unless you have built the necessary administrative infrastructure to run things and you remain aware of what's happening, both in your business and in the marketplace.

3. **Understand the importance of accountability and transparency.**

A lack of accountability and transparency on the part of leadership will ruin a business faster than almost anything. Regrettably, it has become commonplace to read about scandals in the lives of business owners, but those stories typically fail to talk about the consequences for the families of those who acted inappropriately. The damage to the reputations and futures of those in the scandal's wake aren't thought about when one engages in selfish, immature, and often immoral behavior.

There are many options available today to assist business owners with being held accountable for their actions. This is particularly important for someone in a position of authority in a church or Christian-oriented business. The use of accountability tools will help discourage someone from trying to get around certain things, and it will provide evidence that accusations made against them are false if that person is living correctly.

A story is told of Billy Graham when he was in England for an evangelistic crusade. He knew that British TV was allowed to show nudity, so he pulled the TV cable from the wall in his room so he couldn't be tempted to turn it on. I've also heard of business owners who refused to get in an elevator with a member of the opposite sex without someone else with them to avoid the possibility of any accusations being made of something inappropriate taking place.

You may be thinking that these examples are a bit extreme, but we've all heard news stories about professional athletes and how much they spent on their legal defense and the years it took to defeat claims of illegal or inappropriate sexual behavior. Whether the temptations to do wrong are sexual or financial in nature, I'm reminded of an old saying that can be updated this way: "An ounce of accountability and transparency is worth a pound of cure."

4. Understand how to deal with distractions.

A key element of business operations is staying on task and on mission, and that requires dealing with distractions. Face it, distractions are something that business owners and employees alike deal with every day, if not every hour. We live in a world of shiny objects that distract us and take our attention from where it should be. To deal with those distractions, we must establish boundaries that will help us stay focused on the task at hand.

Throughout the workday, we can be bombarded by a variety of distractions, from the sounds of chimes or pings from notifications on our phones or laptops, to hearing the words, "Hey, you got a minute?" All of these must be dealt with by setting firm, and when necessary, strongly-enforced boundaries.

Those boundaries should be built around a clearly-defined end goal which is the "North Star" for your current task that is demanding your attention. This means the leader must clearly define that end goal and then carefully articulate the necessary boundaries to keep everyone focused on the mission of achieving that goal in the desired timeframe.

I read an article about one of the co-founders of Netflix, Marc Randolph, having predetermined that every Tuesday evening would be date night for his wife and him. He didn't want to be described as the guy who was on his seventh startup and seventh marriage, so he set a firm goal of being done with work at 5:00 PM on Tuesdays no matter what. His team quickly realized that if there was a crisis at 4:59 PM, they would have to talk to him about it while he was exiting the building and walking to his car. If it wasn't resolved by the time he got to his car, it would have to wait until Wednesday. That boundary was important to him for having a healthy marriage.

Have you ever encountered someone who had set up those types of boundaries? How does it make you feel when you encounter the boundary and have to wait for them to become available again (like on Wednesday morning) to address something you wanted to deal with at 4:59 PM on Tuesday? Do you understand and respect the boundary, or do you resent it?

If you don't respect that boundary and resent not getting the time you want when you want it, maybe you need to work on your own boundaries and understand the importance of preventing distractions that can take you off the path to success.

One of the best illustrations of this that I know, and I'm sure you are familiar with, is the story of the tortoise and the hare. Multiple distractions kept the hare from easily reaching the end goal of winning the race against the tortoise, whose steady and focused plodding allowed him to achieve the unlikely goal of winning the race against his competitor.

Business Organization

J. C. Penney said, "No business can succeed in any great degree without being properly organized." Boaz not only had well-organized business operations, but he had an organized work structure for his team. In Ruth 2:5, the phrase "servant that was set over the reapers" is used, and in the verses following, Boaz also refers to "the young men" and "maidens" who were in the fields assisting with the harvest. The young men and maidens may have been the ones tasked with looking after the needs of the reapers, like bundling sheaves of grain and bringing them food and water.

Boaz had a detailed, multi-level organizational structure with a clear chain of command. There were the support staff (the young men and maidens) who assisted those producing and collecting the revenue (the reapers) whose work performance was tracked and managed by the overseer who reported to the ultimate leader of the organization (Boaz) and kept him up to date and involved in what was happening.

Organization is the framework in which clear communication can occur. We see this displayed when Boaz first came to the field and saw Ruth. When Boaz asked his overseer who she was, he wasn't disappointed with an "I don't know" response. The fact that the overseer was able to tell him who she was, where she had come from, and who her mother-in-law was shows that Boaz had probably had previous communications with his overseer regarding the need to know who was in his fields, what they were doing, and how they were performing.

The overseer understood what his responsibilities were within the organization and to Boaz himself.

The overseer also had authority delegated to him by Boaz. In the culture of the times, gleaning was a way of providing support for the indigent and foreigners who were willing to work. There would have been some competitive nature in those who wanted to glean, and the overseer would have been given authority to determine who would and would not be allowed to glean in the fields of Boaz.

Because the overseer knew and understood his responsibilities and exercised the authority he had been given, he was able to answer Boaz's simple, direct question. That answer and what resulted from it, which we will discuss further when we look at the legacy of Boaz, impacted history in a major way.

The overseer was part of Boaz's administrative staff. Immediately under his authority were the reapers, those directly responsible for doing the work that produced revenue. Constant stooping and bending to cut the grain made theirs a hard, back-breaking, job. They may also have been the ones given the responsibility of getting the grain to the threshing site and helping to protect it during processing.

At the bottom of the chain, but no less important to the success of Boaz's organization, were those Boaz referred to as the "young men" and "maidens". As their names imply, these were likely ones in their teens who were tasked with the job of assisting those above them in the chain of command. Maybe the young men helped tie the bundles of grain and the maidens made sure everyone had water and food during the harvesting.

Without the support staff, the ones doing the harvesting would not have been able to work nearly as long or accomplish as much.

It certainly appears that Boaz understood the importance of organizational structure and clearly defined roles and responsibilities for those who worked for him.

How can I apply this to my business?

Effective organization management allows for people from various backgrounds with differing personalities to be assembled to work together toward a common goal. Organization gives employees a sense of direction and enables them to understand their roles and responsibilities within the organization as they collectively achieve success.

Boaz's business model highlights the importance of a well-structured organization where each team member, regardless of their role, plays a vital part in overall success. His acknowledgment of the young men and maidens demonstrates that every position, from the lowest to the highest, is essential. This reinforces the idea that a successful business depends not just on leadership but on a cohesive and well-supported team where everyone understands their contributions are valued.

To apply this concept to your business, it's crucial to establish a clear organizational structure with defined roles and responsibilities. This structure ensures that everyone knows their place within the team and how their work impacts the bigger picture. Effective organizational management allows for streamlined operations, where support roles enhance productivity by taking on tasks that enable key players to focus on their primary responsibilities.

Furthermore, defining roles helps prevent confusion and overlap, reducing the risk of inefficiency or burnout. By recognizing the value of every team member, businesses can foster an environment of respect and accountability, which boosts morale and engagement. A well-organized business with clear communication channels can adapt quickly to changes, handle challenges efficiently, and work cohesively toward shared objectives, ultimately driving sustained success.

Business Leadership

It has been said that "leadership is an action, not a position." Good leaders take active roles in what is happening around them. When we are first introduced to Boaz in the Book of Ruth, we quickly see some traits that helped make him an effective leader in his business.

Boaz "inspected what he expected". This is an oft-repeated business slogan, but what does it really mean, and how is it carried out?

As we've already seen, Boaz was not an absentee business owner. Despite being a mighty man of wealth, he chose to be present in and fully aware of his business surroundings and life circumstances. Boaz believed in inspecting what he expected. He came out to see how his harvesters were doing at the beginning of the barley harvest in Bethlehem. There is nothing to suggest that his visit to the field that day was anything other than a regular and welcome event. Absentee or disengaged owners are frequently resented or disrespected.

Boaz looked. The second thing Boaz did when he arrived in the field was to look around and take in what was happening. When he looked, he saw something new and different that he hadn't seen at other barley harvests. He was familiar with how things should look. He saw something new. This made him ask questions.

Boaz listened as the overseer answered his specific question regarding who that woman was that he hadn't seen in his field before.

By being observant and looking at his surroundings and then by listening to what others were telling him about what was happening, **Boaz learned** information that enabled him to make wise decisions.

Boaz then led the situation by giving clear instructions to his overseer, to the other servants and the young men, to the reapers, and to Ruth herself regarding her status, work opportunity, and the generosity he wanted to show her.

The events that were set in motion as a result of Boaz's arrival in the field that day are direct results of his leadership actions. Leadership requires one to be at certain places at certain times to make sure things are going according to plan. Boaz was in the right place at the right time to observe and learn important information and give direction to the team accordingly.

Boaz lingered. He didn't just walk away from the situation. He stayed at the field and shared lunch with his team to make sure his communications were understood and followed by all.

How can I apply this to my business?

We often see news clips of politicians doing photo-op visits at various places like restaurants and factories or at disaster sites. While some genuinely engage with those around them and become involved in the situation, others simply smile and go through the motions. To the discerning eye, the differences between those two types of leadership styles can be seen. One is clearly for political optics which they hope will be spun correctly in the eyes of the public, and the other is a true leader who is leading from the front by being willing to go to the difficult areas, not just the comfortable ones, and inspect things firsthand.

Just think about our country's southern border or places that have been devastated by a hurricane, flood or fire and the various responses we've seen to these things.

As an Ohio resident, I saw a definite lack of business and political leadership showing up at the horrible train crash site in East Palestine, Ohio. A then-newly-elected U.S. Senator from Ohio is to be commended for showing up and being physically present in that town more than the senior U.S. Senator from our state.

Knowing what is going on firsthand isn't just for politicians. It's critical for business owners as well. Just being in a place isn't enough. You have to really look at what is happening by breaking away from your schedule or agenda. To really learn and not just be seen, you have to carefully observe what is happening around you.

I remember reading a story about a former CEO, now deceased, of the Coca-Cola Company who would go to various locations and stop mid-stride to ask why there wasn't a Coca-Cola vending machine in that location. That leader wasn't just there to be seen. He was observing his surroundings and looking for opportunities to grow and develop the company.

When a leader is present and making observations, it leads to asking questions, which leads to new information, which leads to potential new opportunities, decisions, or developments in business that can have a very profound effect on the company. Others in the company will then begin to look at things as well and ask themselves what is new, what is different, and what can be improved.

In addition to looking, a good leader will listen. It has been said that God gave us two ears and two eyes but only one mouth, so we need to spend at least 80% of our time listening and looking and only 20% of our time talking.

Good listening isn't only about *what* is said, but *how* it's said. We see this frequently when questions are asked of political leaders. The questions are actually political, business, or economic statements being made by the one asking the question. A good leader can listen to the question, cut through the noise, redirect as necessary, and give an answer that stays on target. Just listen to how questions are answered in a political debate or news conference. Does the person fall for the trap, or do they stay on message? Do they correct the questioner if that person is asking the question the wrong way, and is it done in a polite but clear manner? Being able to do this requires listening and responding appropriately, not just speaking whatever comes to your mind.

Looking at a situation and listening to what is being said leads to learning. Sometimes that learning is for the purpose of validating that the systems you have in place in your business are working correctly or need to be adjusted.

Sometimes learning is so you can adapt to change or even completely redo things in a time of crisis.

One of the greatest leadership examples we've seen is that of former New York City Mayor Rudy Giuliani after the terrible 9/11 terrorist attacks. Mayor Giuliani was physically present at the World Trade Center site as much as possible despite the physical risk because he understood that he needed to be present to look, listen, and learn for himself what was really happening.

Learning is incredibly important in fluid business situations. A business leader who sits at a desk and merely looks at spreadsheets, reports, and memos is going to have a completely different opinion of where things stand in their business than one who gets out and walks through the company listening and talking to employees. Great insight can be gained by listening not just to *what* your employees are saying, but by hearing *how* they are saying it. Pay attention to their tone and how long the conversations last. This type of direct, engaged learning will enable a business owner to lead from a better, more informed, and therefore, more powerful position. Knowledge is power, so learning by looking and listening is crucial to a successful business endeavor.

Good leadership also involves education.

President Harry S. Truman said, "Not all readers are leaders, but all leaders are readers." Well-read, well-educated leaders can take the information they learn, turn it into educational content, and communicate it to the team so that everyone understands the mission and goals of the organization.

When these actions are taken, you, as a business owner, are then able to lead effectively and make good business decisions. You will have the information you need to reinforce what is working right, make adjustments that may be needed, or even make major changes.

While writing this book, I am engaged with others in aggressively leading a significant business opportunity as major changes need to be made. I've learned that one of the most important leadership questions to ask in critical situations is, "What am I not being told, and what do I need to know?" Sometimes what is missing is more important than the information you are given.

Once you have that answer, the question that logically follows is, "Why is it missing, and what do I do about it?" Our human tendency is not to discuss or disclose painful or awkward information, so a business leader can be easily duped by someone who is not giving all the information about a situation.

This reinforces the importance of looking, listening, and learning so you can figure out what you may be missing or are not being told. This interventional leadership is crucial to correcting a growing problem before it gets out of control and threatens the viability of your entire enterprise.

A forward-looking leader also needs to look, listen, and learn about what is going on with external factors that influence their business. You must be aware of things like the ever-changing interest rates and inflation, and major demographic changes that are underway due to the aging baby-boom generation and how all these things impact various aspects of your life and business, including investments. For the past few decades, baby boomers have been pouring money into their retirement savings accounts, and those at the tail end of that generation will soon be drawing money out of those accounts. That will change business dynamics because these individuals will become more conservative consumers and investors. Good leaders are already looking, listening, and learning with those economic trends in mind.

One final point I want to make about good leaders is that they linger. By that I mean they don't just give orders. They are involved and working alongside their team to accomplish a task. For example, a business owner who wants his company and employees to be a help to the community doesn't just tell everyone that they will be volunteering to help at a soup kitchen. A good business leader will be standing behind the food table serving those who come through the line and engaging with them, not just for a quick photo op, but because their heart is truly in the task. Real leaders will linger and do what needs to be done when the situation isn't about money, fame, or reputation for themselves.

I think of Lt. Michael Murphy and the reports of his heroism in Afghanistan when he and three other Navy Seals were surrounded by overwhelming forces. This posthumous recipient of the Congressional Medal of Honor was so engaged in what he was doing that he took risks on himself which ultimately cost him his life so he could save the lives of his team members. That type of committed, passionate engagement in what you are doing is the result of being present so you can look, listen, learn, and lead.

Business Communications
A critical element of any successful business is great communication. While this is important even if your business has only one employee, it is even more important if your organization has multiple levels and employees in its organizational structure. The operation run by Boaz would certainly fit into the latter category.

When we first see Boaz as he arrives in the field to check on the progress of the barley harvest, we immediately see a demonstration of communication based on mutual respect between Boaz and the reapers who worked for him.

"Boaz...said unto the reapers, The Lord be with you. And they answered him, The Lord bless thee." Boaz was the man at the top of the chain of command. He could have ignored the reapers all together and simply addressed the overseer, but he didn't. He was polite and respectful to those on his team, and he in turn received politeness and respect back.

"Without appreciation and respect for other people, true leadership becomes ineffective, if not impossible." The truth in this quote attributed to George Foreman is one that business owners must embrace if they want to be successful. Boaz obviously understood this, and more importantly, he clearly and publicly communicated his respect and appreciation to those in his employ by his words and actions. His talk matched his walk.

Not only did he show respect to those working the field, but his greeting and their response also demonstrated a reverence for God and exemplified what would be written many years later by the Apostle Paul in Colossians 3:17 when he reminded us that whatever we do "in word or deed, do all in the name of the Lord Jesus." We get a sense that there was unity and balance among them in that they were all working together toward a common goal, and they were doing it in an organized manner and in a way that was respectful both to God and others. They were all working "heartily as unto the Lord, and not unto men." This is stewardship and leadership in action.

Having that attitude toward work changes everything about one's work ethic and desire to do a good job. Boaz and his organization understood the importance of the barley harvest in that culture. They had recently come out of a long period of famine. This harvest was a business opportunity they could not afford to lose. Establishing and clarifying lines and methods of communication before a crucial meeting or event is a hallmark of a good business leader.

When we read Chapter 2 of the Book of Ruth and look at what was said during this encounter Boaz had with all those in the field that day, we see him clearly communicating his instructions relative to the change occasioned by Ruth gleaning in his field. He made it clear to the entire organization that Ruth was to be given the opportunity to glean and that she was granted access to the water and food that was set aside for the reapers, the young men, and the maidens. Boaz made sure his workers not only understood the "what" and the "why", but he stayed long enough to make sure the "when" was understood as well, that she was allowed to glean daily throughout the remainder of the barley and wheat harvests.

Boaz didn't rely solely on his team to communicate his wishes to Ruth. He used direct, one-on-one communication to ask her to stay with his team and glean only in his fields. Boaz made sure Ruth knew that he had already given instructions to the others that she was not to be hassled or turned away from gleaning in his fields. He wanted his instructions to be clearly communicated to Ruth.

This clear, direct, and consistent communication meant there was no risk of that important information being distorted, accidentally or intentionally, as it worked its way down the chain of command.

By Boaz taking the extra time and effort to make his instructions clear to all members of his team at the same time, he was also reducing the risk of questions and gossip about Ruth. It would have been easy for someone on his team to see Ruth as a foreign beggar and resent her. His team, however, had heard the instructions in the boss's own words. The idea of granting a foreigner access to the food and water that had been prepared for the workers was highly unusual in the culture of that time. It was through clear communication in word and actions that the team understood what Boaz was expecting and the generosity he was displaying.

How can I apply this to my business?

Whenever I address the issue of communication, I feel I am standing in front of a mirror preaching to myself. It's that feeling you get when you realize that while you may be pointing a finger at someone else, there are three fingers pointing back at you.

Communication in business needs to be respectful and clear. If it's true that "to be clear is to be kind," then not being clear in our communication is being unkind. Let's clarify this statement a bit further. What exactly is meant by "clear"?

Here is an acronym to help make it **CLEAR** for you:

C – Consistent: Your communication and message must be consistent. A lack of consistency will lead to confusion. Confusion leads to lost opportunities, or worse.

L – Logical: What you say must make sense in the context of the communication and situation. If what you say isn't consistent and logical, it can leave people wondering what you are really talking about. Be on message! One of the best ways to verify that your message is on point, clear and logical is to ask those receiving your communication what questions they have. This should be done in a manner that elicits honest feedback to avoid the bias of a feedback loop.

E – Engaging: If your message does not capture the attention of the ones hearing it, the likelihood of them listening to it, understanding it, accepting it, and acting on it goes way down. In this age of technology, engagement is a real challenge given the many ways in which it can occur. No longer is communication done primarily face to face or via a phone call as it was decades ago. We now communicate using email, text messaging, video meetings on platforms such as Zoom, and through various social media and instant messaging apps we have on our phones. Some of these methods don't allow the tone or intensity behind the words being communicated to come through. Volume, pitch, tone, and rate of speech are important parts of verbal communication. When communication is delivered in writing, you have to give considerable thought to the subject line/headline used and the specific words you use to draw and hold the attention of the readers.

A – Accurate: Communication that is accurate is of paramount importance! Are the facts and information being conveyed – dates, times, locations, names, persons, and objectives – correct?

R – Relatable: Your communication must be relevant to the audience receiving it so they can understand and relate to what you want them to know, think or feel.

In the press of day-to-day matters, our communication is often too brief. In comedy, brevity may be the soul of wit, but in business, incomplete or unclear communication is usually rather costly. In the case of Boaz and Ruth, what if Ruth had assumed that Boaz was saying she should stay with his maidens just because he was "being polite", so she didn't show up the next day?

Clear communication requires multiple instances of giving the same, consistent message. Communicate abundantly! Give an overwhelming amount of communication about a particular item or project if necessary. When it comes to communication, less is not more.

I know so many business leaders who are brilliant visionaries. They spend a great deal of time thinking through ideas and processing the steps necessary to bring their visions to life, but they forget that they now have to clearly communicate that entire thought process to their team so their team can catch up with them and have the understanding they need to take the ball and advance the project. It's incredibly frustrating for team members to receive communication from a leader when that communication is missing vital data as to what to do next and how to do it.

I remember having a conversation with someone who shared with me how their employer would send them incomplete communications regarding some new project. The incomplete communications were the result of the enthusiasm of the leader causing them to go too fast and not share all relevant information with the team members, particularly the administrative assistants, as to what needed to be done. The leader was leaving out important information like full names, addresses, and other contact information their team members needed to complete their tasks. The leader was so focused on the success of the sale they closed and getting on to the next one that they forgot about providing the necessary data the back office needed to fulfill their responsibilities.

One of the biggest causes of unclear communication is the assumption by a leader or team member that a message has actually been received. A task doesn't get completed or the ball gets dropped somewhere in the process, and the response from the one who thought they had communicated is, "But I sent you an email!"

This may come as a shock to some of you, but simply "sending" an email or text message is not "communication". Communication truly occurs when an email or text message has received a response that is appropriate and substantive to the content in the outgoing message. For example, you send an email to someone on your team that says, "The meeting has been moved from 11:30 AM to 9:00 AM." You then receive a reply that reads, "Understood. See you at 9:00 AM." That's when you know that communication has occurred. If you send your email about the changed meeting time and get no reply, don't expect the recipient to show up at 9:00. It's possible they will, but don't expect it.

I'm not suggesting that all emails be sent with a "read receipt" because that encumbers things and makes it look like there is a "gotcha" somewhere in the email. It's much better to follow up with the message recipient via a different method of communication. Maybe you send them a brief text or give them a call. Using multiple methods makes it more likely that the message will be received and understood, and that communication has ultimately occurred.

I'm reminded of something that happened once when I was traveling to Texas on business for a relatively new organization. There was some incomplete and unclear communication between other members of that organization as to whether one of the members would be flying into the airport in Laredo or the one in San Antonio. This unclear communication resulted in one of the leaders of the organization waiting for hours at the wrong airport for the other member to arrive. To clarify the communication and locate the missing member, multiple phone calls had to be made from people in Laredo and San Antonio, and even from someone in Washington, DC.

While the airport mix-up was an inconvenience, crisis situations can happen for many reasons and usually at unexpected times. It could be a national disaster like 9/11, a worldwide epidemic (flashbacks to Covid?), or a natural disaster like a hurricane, flood or fire. On a more personal level, you could have a major adverse business event or accident happen, or you unexpectedly find yourself as a defendant in a lawsuit.

During times of crisis, clarity in your communication is even more critical. I have had many opportunities to help clients through a variety of crisis situations, and one thing I've noticed that sets a true leader apart from those who are still learning how to lead is their ability to remain calm and provide clear information to their team regarding knowledge of the situation and instructions as to what needs to be done.

We saw many examples of this during the Covid shutdowns. Businesses that held meetings and shared the facts with their employees – information regarding cash, receivables, their ability to continue operating if no money was coming in, the strategic maneuvering that would have to take place in the company – were the ones most likely to survive the shutdowns.

Whatever the nature of the crisis, clear, honest communication with all employees helps eliminate any surprises, rumors, or thoughts of there being some hidden agenda. It develops unity and focus among the team members and leads to the sharing of ideas that can make it easier for the company to weather the storm. During the Covid shutdowns, there were some businesses that made a complete shift in the marketing of their products and services to make it easier for customers who would be struggling financially but needed those things. As a result, some of these companies experienced growth in their sales because they adjusted to the situation, and that adjustment began with the leadership standing before the company and clearly articulating what needed to be done, why it needed to be done, and the resource base from which it would be done.

If you want to see some examples of good communication during a crisis, go to YouTube and find videos of Rudy Giuliani speaking to the press after 9/11 or videos of former Vice President Mike Pence speaking at the beginning of the Covid shutdowns. While their language may seem very elementary, it was designed to be understood by anyone. It was so important during those times that someone in that leadership role was able to articulate the necessary messages so clearly and confidently.

I'm sure we can also think of "leaders" whose communication, in times of crisis, becomes terse and incomplete, leaving their colleagues, team members, vendors, etc., confused as to what to do and how to do it. When there is a looming deadline, time is wasted when key people must search for information that their leader was either unable or unwilling to clearly provide. This is a huge drag on the business when it comes to efficiency and operations. It also damages morale and builds layers of cynicism in those whose minds and hearts have left the company long before their bodies have.

It's important to remember that during times of crisis, the recipients of your communications have a lot going on in their minds. Fear may be heightened which can affect their thinking, perception and memory, so extra time and clarity with repetition is essential to make your messages understood. Calmness, clarity, and conciseness, along with an action plan, give the recipients a level of comfort so they can move forward in the challenging environment.

I remember listening to a live broadcast years ago as a tornado was passing through Moore, Oklahoma. A national news service got a local news reporter on the line to get real-time information about what was happening. This was the reporter's opportunity to demonstrate clear communication in a time of crisis. People from across the nation were listening for information and descriptions of what the reporter was seeing on the ground, as he was going to be the eyes and ears of America.

Unfortunately, the reporter got so emotional and began speaking so rapidly that he hyperventilated, and most of the words coming out of his mouth were either unintelligible or focused on his own personal safety. Those are human emotions that any of us might feel in that situation, but when you are in a leadership position that requires communication during a crisis, you must be able to step back from your personal emotions and concerns so you can focus on the bigger picture.

I'm not judging that reporter because he had not signed up to be the equivalent of a combat journalist, but he provides an important illustration. As the tornado was passing through that town, information he could have provided as to the size of the tornado, the direction it was heading, and maybe specific information as to what streets or identifiable landmarks it was approaching would have been very helpful.

If you find yourself in such a time of crisis, for example, having to call 911 because someone at your business has been injured or something bad has happened to your office or building, discipline your mind to slow down so you can clearly communicate the information a 911 dispatcher needs to hear. Make sure you are the good leader your team needs at that moment.

Business Culture

Company culture is the backbone of any successful organization. It is the set of values, attitudes and practices that enable a company to do what it does while creating a positive experience for its employees and customers. If we study the relationships among Boaz, his team, and Ruth, we can see how Boaz demonstrated three key aspects of a healthy, diverse company culture.

The first thing that stands out is his **acceptance of those who were different**. Ruth recognized this and told Boaz how grateful she was that he had spoken kindly to her even though she wasn't like the other handmaids in the field (Ruth 2:13). Ruth was from Moab, a people who were perpetual enemies of Israel and whose religious practices involved idolatry and even human sacrifices. She had left her culture and religion behind in Moab and converted to Judaism, but many would still have considered Ruth an outsider. She was different from the other women in appearance, she probably still wore clothing that reflected her Moabite heritage, and she would have spoken Hebrew haltingly and with a different accent, since it was a second language for her.

Many might have looked at Ruth and immediately written her off as an "evil Moabite woman" because of where she was from, but that wasn't how Boaz saw her. We are told that he knew her full story and how she cared for her mother-in-law and now loved and worshipped the same God he did. He let her know that he realized how difficult it must have been for her to leave her home and come to a strange place. He accepted Ruth based on her character, behavior and who she was as a person rather than dismissing her because of her looks, ethnic heritage or her past.

The second key thing we see in Boaz's business culture is that he **judged others on their character and work ethic**. If Boaz were in business today, he would be known as an "equal opportunity employer". While he was accepting of those who were different, it doesn't appear that he allowed those differences to affect what he expected from those who were in his employ or who gleaned in his fields. Boaz understood that it was more important to give people an equal opportunity to work and help themselves instead of giving them handouts. He recognized the self-worth element in human beings that makes us feel better about receiving things we work for and earn rather than what is just handed to us for nothing.

Diversity was accepted as long as the work was accomplished. The overall goal of the enterprise of harvesting crops to feed and sustain people was not sacrificed in order to celebrate diversity. The goal was the unifier. Unity in their work resulted from cohesive organizational structure and clear, consistent communication.

Ruth had clearly captured the attention of Boaz that day when he visited his field, although no mention is made regarding her looks. He could simply have instructed someone on his team to give Ruth a basket full of grain, so she didn't have to do the backbreaking work of gathering it for herself, but he chose not to. He gave her an opportunity to provide for herself and Naomi instead of giving her a free handout.

While it is true that he instructed the reapers to drop some handfuls on purpose for her to gather, it could be that he wanted to see what kind of work ethic she really had. Would she work all day and gather all she could, or would she get tired and quit as soon as she felt she had done enough?

What Boaz learned was that Ruth had good character and a strong work ethic. When given an opportunity, she exceeded the standard he had set.

Having a **genuine concern for the welfare of his workers and the gleaners** was another key element of Boaz's business culture. We learn from chapter 2 of the Book of Ruth that the reapers and even the gleaners had a place of shelter where they could go and rest (verse 7). Boaz made sure the workers had what they needed when it came to food and water (verses 9 and 14). Heatstroke or similar concerns were a real issue given the climate and time of year. Workplace safety was as important as performance.

Boaz made sure that Ruth knew she was welcome to join the others to rest and take her meals, even giving her corn when he himself joined them for a meal. It seems that Boaz was involved with those under his authority. Picture in your mind a meal in the shade near an open field shared by an older wealthy man, his overseer, multiple youthful day laborers of both sexes, and a foreign-looking young lady. Joining the workers for a meal may have been a regular occurrence for Boaz. It certainly would have given him the chance to hear from them as to any ideas or concerns they might have had. It also reinforced his prior communication as to the opportunity being given to Ruth, and his actions reinforced his words.

Boaz may have been ahead of his time when it comes to maintaining a safe and appropriate work environment for the women and girls. We see nothing but respect for Ruth being demonstrated by Boaz, and he demanded the same thing from those working with her. Harassment was not tolerated, and Boaz gave explicit instructions to the young men that they were not to touch her. It was not uncommon for women to be molested in the fields. We see Naomi allude to this fact in verse 22 of chapter 2 when she expresses her gratefulness that Ruth has found her way into the fields of a man like Boaz, and she instructs Ruth to stay with the maidens of Boaz just as Boaz had asked Ruth to do. Naomi recognized God's hand of protection on Ruth.

We are given enough information to draw a clear conclusion when it comes to the business culture and work environment Boaz cultivated among his team: respect for each of those who were part of his team was a top priority. This culture of acceptance and concern for the safety and provision of all the workers as well as concern for her welfare kept Ruth in the fields of Boaz until the end of the harvest. Neither she nor the other workers had any need to go elsewhere.

It was not until Ruth went home to Naomi after her first day of gleaning that she learned the whole story of who Boaz was and what that might mean for them.

Naomi knew the end of the harvests would come soon, and she was ready with a plan. The future of Boaz was about to change as well.

How can I apply this to my business?

Do you operate from a culture that allows for divine influence? By that I mean do you create an environment in which ethical and moral principles guide decision making? It's about leading with integrity, empathy, and a sense of greater purpose.

It's essential to build a culture that values every individual, promotes safety, and fosters respect. A positive work environment goes beyond just avoiding negative behaviors; it actively encourages supportive interactions and the well-being of all employees.

This includes implementing policies that protect workers from harassment, discrimination, and unsafe conditions.

Regrettably, workplace sexual harassment and violence is a major problem in our culture. That evil can devastate the lives of people in so many ways, particularly when it is perpetrated by an owner of a business upon a vulnerable employee. The long-term legal, economic, moral and spiritual consequences are so costly and devastating, you would think that nobody in their right mind would commit acts of workplace sexual violence.

You might think using the word "violence" is too strong, but I would argue that it isn't from the eyes of the victim and their family and children who depend on them.

It is incumbent upon a leader and business owner to make sure their company is a safe place to work for both women and men. The news is filled with stories of how men have overstepped their bounds, and as a result, they have had to face the consequences for their inappropriate actions toward women.

We do not sin in a vacuum.

The consequences for our actions not only affect us, but they have far-reaching effects on our families, our children, our coworkers and colleagues, our employees, our customers, and even on our future marketing messages.

In our society, particularly in the media, there is a desire to spread these salacious stories so they can grab attention and clicks from those who read them. You cannot give any room to that kind of behavior!

No matter the size of your company, one of the most important things you can do when it comes to sexual misconduct in the workplace is to make sure there is accountability for anyone who is reported for their inappropriate behavior, and that the reporting process is seen to be objective and has been made as easy and comfortable as possible.

For example, think about a family-owned business in which the Human Resources Department is headed up by a family member of the owner. How is an employee who is receiving unwanted advances from another family member in the company going to be able to report that in a way in which they will be heard and believed and have the confidence that the matter will be taken seriously?

This is a good time to address another issue that is related to having and maintaining the proper workplace culture. Obviously, this area is not covered in the Book of Ruth by Boaz because electronics and the internet didn't exist at that time. Employees who have been given company-owned devices (phones, tablets, computers, etc.) need to fully acknowledge their understanding of the fact that how they use those devices, particularly when on the internet, will be monitored by the company.

This means that an employee who uses a company device to access inappropriate websites, such as pornography or gambling websites, for example, will be properly disciplined. It is completely inappropriate for a company to permit its equipment and electronic devices to be used for any type of inappropriate, illegal, or immoral activity.

It is a well-known fact that many employees use company devices, particularly computers, to carry out personal activities completely unrelated to their job. That's how we got the term "Cyber Monday". It was noted that on the Monday after Black Friday, there was a significant increase in online purchases because people were looking for good deals on goods left over from the big Thanksgiving weekend shopping promotions.

For many, it was an opportunity to do online shopping once they were back at work where they had a good internet connection. The term has become part of our culture and is now another huge day of sales for businesses.

How a company chooses to regulate and monitor the usage of company devices is an important decision that needs to be clearly communicated in writing to all employees who must acknowledge their understanding of the rules. It may be fine for an employee to use their computer on a break or lunch hour to check their email or make Amazon purchases, but any use of the computer for things that are destructive, harmful, or inappropriate for the workplace needs to be prohibited, and the consequences for violating the guidelines need to be clearly spelled out and disciplinary actions followed through.

There also needs to be an understanding regarding the use of your personal devices, particularly your personal cell phone, to carry out work-related activities. Employees must realize that should they choose to use their personal cell phones for business purposes, like logging into company email accounts or sending work-related text messages, there is the risk that their personal cell phone may become evidence in a business litigation case.

A prudent business owner will recognize this and put the appropriate protections in place by supplying employees with company-owned devices for use in business activities. Employees can then keep what is personal separate from what is work-related.

In the event an electronic discovery becomes relevant because of civil or criminal litigation involving the company, the business owner would be well advised to meet with an expert in the field regarding setting up parameters for protecting privacy while securing information.

Boaz's commitment to maintaining a safe and respectful working environment reflects a forward-thinking approach to business culture, particularly concerning the treatment of women and vulnerable individuals. Creating the right culture in your business will help ensure a strong, unified team working toward a shared vision, just as Boaz did with his workers.

"An ounce of accountability and transparency is worth a pound of cure."

Applying Boaz to Strategy:
The Kira Golden Interview - Part 2

Jeff Watson: So we see Ruth on day one of the barley harvest, and Naomi says from day two on, "You stick with what Boaz said, God bless you." And then the next time we see her, she's consistently done what she's supposed to do. Then it comes time for the threshing of the barley, and there's the encounter on the threshing floor. That, once again, goes back to what you already talked about. I want you to elaborate on where Naomi is coaching Ruth on what to do.

Kira Golden: Well, I'll be honest—this part of the story has always been a bit puzzling to me. I'm still not sure I fully understand it. But what I'm starting to grasp is that Ruth's success in business—if you want to call it that—wouldn't have happened without the obedience and generosity of Boaz. And I think we often overlook the importance of those who make a way for us. Another thing that really strikes me is that Boaz never advanced on Ruth. And that's huge when you think about women in business. There's often this undercurrent or even explicit expectation that you owe something to the men who have helped or opened doors for you. But Boaz didn't do that. His actions and heart were pure, and that's key to understanding what was happening there. Boaz was humble, working hard, and sleeping on the threshing floor—basically, he was all in, not taking it easy or delegating.

Jeff Watson: It's a crucial time in the business, and he's there, sleeping at the plant.

Kira Golden: Exactly. He's in it, not sitting back waiting for reports. And when Ruth presents herself at his feet, it's such a humble and probably scary moment for her. But again, it speaks to Naomi's coaching and Ruth's trust in her guidance. Ruth had worked in Boaz's fields and felt safe. That safety is crucial.

Jeff Watson: I go back to day one in the field. Boaz specifically told everyone to leave her alone.

Kira Golden: Yeah, that's true.

Jeff Watson: He made it clear. He told his men to leave her alone. But he also practiced what he preached.

Kira Golden: Yes, exactly.

Jeff Watson: And that's something you pointed out that I hadn't really picked up on. Boaz told his guys to leave her alone, and he did the same. He didn't make any advances on her. Ruth came to him as Naomi had coached her.

Kira Golden: Right. And it's interesting because, even though things are different today, I'm not sure they've changed all that much. The whole transaction wasn't just about redeeming Naomi's land—it was about redeeming Naomi's family and offering herself up in marriage and partnership. It wasn't just romantic or relational—it was also business. Back then, women didn't just go out and buy land or run businesses. Ruth had a lot to offer, both as Naomi's daughter-in-law and in her own right. She brought value to the table.

Jeff Watson: I've got to give a shout-out to Naomi here. This conversation with you has opened my eyes to an aspect I hadn't seen before. Naomi strategized this whole thing. She told Ruth how to dress, where to go, what to say. Naomi's thinking three moves ahead, making sure not only that Boaz redeems the land but also that Ruth marries him, securing the future for their family.

Kira Golden: Yeah, Naomi was definitely thinking generationally.

Jeff Watson: Three generations ahead, right? And I think Boaz was thinking ahead, too, but Naomi was just as strategic.

Kira Golden: For sure. We talked earlier about power and character, and in this story, we see God working in unseen realms—parallel paths, really. Boaz was doing his thing, and Naomi and Ruth were doing theirs. Their processes were aligned, whether they knew it or not. Boaz was this great protector, but Ruth wasn't just some helpless woman needing to be saved. She was hardworking, and she carried her own weight. In many ways, she was Boaz's equal—different, but equal in character and spirit.

Jeff Watson: Absolutely true.

Kira Golden: Yeah, different in gender and in how things showed up for them, but equal in the deeper sense.

Jeff Watson: And Boaz noticed that. He said, "You've been an amazing worker; you haven't gone after younger men." He admired her character.

Kira Golden: Yeah, exactly.

Jeff Watson: Now, here's a question I'm still trying to figure out. After Ruth goes back home with extra bounty that Boaz gives her, Naomi asks her, "Who are you?" Not "How did it go?" but "Who are you?" Like, "Are you engaged? What's your status?"

Kira Golden: What happens next?

Jeff Watson: Ruth tells Naomi everything that happened, and Naomi says, "Wait here. Boaz will take care of everything today." Then Boaz goes to the city gates early in the morning to set up his business plan.

Kira Golden: That's an interesting detail. The "Who are you?" question really strikes me. It feels like it's about more than just her status—it's about her identity. I'd need to study more deeply, maybe dive into the Hebrew or get some more context, but it's intriguing.

It reminds me of when you asked me earlier, "Who are you?" not "What do you do?" It's deeper than just the surface-level stuff.

Jeff Watson: And then Naomi tells Ruth, "Wait here. It'll happen today." Boaz is handling everything.

Kira Golden: Yeah, that waiting is such a big theme, especially when we talk about women in business. Waiting isn't passive. It's an active, powerful thing, especially after you've made your move. If Ruth had panicked or tried to rush things, it could have disrupted Boaz's plan.

Jeff Watson: I think it would've blown the whole thing up.

Kira Golden: Exactly. The waiting creates a more sustainable outcome. If Ruth had gone running around town, it could've changed everything.

Jeff Watson: Waiting isn't passive, especially after a calculated, powerful move. You wait on God to do His part because you've done all you can do. I think that's a powerful point. Then we see Boaz go to the city gates, wait for the other relative, and in front of witnesses, he sets up the negotiation. He says, "You can redeem the land." The guy says he will, and then Boaz drops the second part— you have to marry Ruth. The guy backs out, and Boaz steps up.

Kira Golden: If Ruth had been out there making noise, that whole delicate negotiation might have gone sideways.

Jeff Watson: Boaz made sure everything was done right, and when it was over, Ruth became his wife. They had a son, Obed. Naomi's now popular, and the women of the town congratulate her, saying Ruth is better to her than seven sons. That speaks volumes about Ruth's character.

Kira Golden: And Naomi's too.

Jeff Watson: Right. And then Ruth and Boaz have Obed, who fathers Jesse, who fathers David. And that lineage leads directly to Jesus Christ.

Kira Golden: Not even that far back—Ruth is David's great-grandmother. That's not many generations.

Jeff Watson: Exactly. And you see how their character and choices set the stage for generations to come. It's all encoded in the family lineage.

Kira Golden: Yeah, the choices we make today carry through our generations, shaping our family dynamics.

Jeff Watson: And that's not just a business thing—it's life. Any final thoughts about Ruth or how her story impacts your perspective on business?

Kira Golden: I think the big takeaway for me is that Ruth's success wasn't just about her work ethic or character—those things were important, but her success also came through her partnership with Boaz. Today, we talk a lot about traditional family values, but historically, women worked, ran businesses, and played key roles in their communities, just like Ruth did. Boaz protected Ruth, but it was her humility, kindness, and willingness to work hard that made their partnership strong. They weren't pushing their own agendas—they were creating opportunities together.

Jeff Watson: That's a great point. When Boaz first asked about Ruth, the overseer said she was a hard worker. That's the first thing Boaz learns about her—her work ethic.

Kira Golden: Exactly. From the start, she presented herself as a partner, not just someone in need of help. Her work ethic, character, and values made her an equal to Boaz in the ways that mattered.

Jeff Watson: It's interesting that even in the Garden of Eden, before sin entered the picture, Adam and Eve worked together. It wasn't about one leading and the other following—it was about partnership.

Kira Golden: Exactly. They worked side by side. The leadership role was about responsibility, not dominance. And that's what we see with Boaz and Ruth. He takes on the harder parts of the responsibility, but it's a shared vision they're working toward.

Jeff Watson: I love that—shared goals. They figured out their strengths and weaknesses and decided together how to move forward.

Kira Golden: Yeah, it makes me think about what "traditional" really means. There's a version of "traditional" where the man is the head of the household in a way that's almost oppressive, and then there's the biblical model, where the man leads by taking on the greater responsibility to serve and execute the shared vision. Boaz wasn't just looking for a wife—he was looking for a partner.

Jeff Watson: Boaz knew Ruth and Naomi would outlive him, and he had to make sure they could continue executing his vision. That shows how much trust he had in Ruth.

Kira Golden: Absolutely. He trusted her to carry it forward.

Jeff Watson: And we see that she did. From Boaz and Ruth to Obed, to Jesse, and eventually to David. And that's a whole other conversation. We could talk about David for hours, but we'll leave it here. This has been a blast—thanks, Kira.

Kira Golden: Thanks, Jeff.

Chapter 4: His Future

"Boaz understood how important it was to own income-producing real estate, and he understood how mergers and acquisitions worked."

At the conclusion of the barley and wheat harvests, which would have taken a total of 60-90 days, a pivotal moment happened in the lives of Boaz and Ruth which was orchestrated, in part, by Naomi. It takes place when Boaz was at the threshing floor where the grain was being winnowed and made ready for sale. This was referenced earlier, but let's look at it a bit more closely.

There are two important reasons which probably brought Boaz to the threshing floor. For one thing, it was the culmination of those harvests, so Boaz probably wanted to be there to observe and measure the success that his business had achieved. The other reason, however, that he may have been there himself was due to security concerns. If ever there were an ideal time for a marauding band of robbers to visit this area of Bethlehem and attack, this would be it. The hard work had been completed, and the grain was now in its most transportable form, making it easy to steal. If you look at Israel's history, you will see that this had been a cultural problem for the previous one hundred years or so. While we don't see much in chapter 3 that points to specific business activity, the events that took place there had a profound impact on the futures of both Boaz and Ruth.

Apparently, it was well known where Boaz would be at this time because Naomi gave Ruth instructions regarding how her culture handled making the request she wanted Ruth to make of Boaz. Acting on that information, Ruth discreetly and appropriately made her request that Boaz act as the kinsman-redeemer on behalf of both her and Naomi.

In Israel's culture at this time, when a person "sold" their farmland, it was really more of a lease or rental agreement, as the one selling the land had the right to buy it back by paying off the remaining years of the lease before the next year of jubilee (which was every 50th year), at which time all property reverted to the family of the original owner. Since the selling party rarely had the funds with which to buy the land back, it often fell to a family member to make the investment. As widows with no children, the land belonging to Elimelech could be redeemed and would then belong to Naomi. Upon Naomi's passing, it would belong to Ruth.

Boaz was aware of the tactical situation involving the redemption of the farmland that Naomi and her late husband had sold prior to moving to Moab. We typically think of Boaz as a farmer, but in reality, he was primarily a real estate investor whose wealth came from his real estate holdings and the income produced from their cash crops. He knew that the only way to get this land into his family tree was to marry Ruth and have a child with her.

The relatives of Boaz may have been disappointed by what took place. Since we are assuming that Boaz had no children prior to marrying Ruth, according to Jewish law, when Boaz died, all the land he owned would go to his siblings, if any, or to his cousins, which he must have had since there was a kinsman nearer to Elimelech than Boaz was. The transaction regarding Elimelech's land had many long-term economic ramifications. It wasn't just a simple love story.

When he was startled awake in the middle of the night and found Ruth lying at his feet so she could make her request, he was able to explain to her that he would do what she was asking regarding redeeming the land, but there was another person who was a nearer kinsman and, therefore, had a higher priority or claim to exercise the right of redemption. Boaz told Ruth that if this other kinsman wished to redeem the land, they would let him do it, but if he wasn't willing, then Boaz would do it. This may have allowed Ruth to sleep well that night knowing that Naomi's land would be redeemed, giving her the rights to the land which would ultimately pass to Ruth.

What does this have to do with Boaz and his real estate investing? He understood how important it was to own income-producing real estate, and he understood how mergers and acquisitions worked. He knew what was required to gain the land, and he knew who his potential competitors were. It's interesting to note that we don't see any discussion about the financial resources of Boaz or his ability to perform the part of a kinsman-redeemer. It was a given since he was a man of wealth, plus he had just harvested and sold a barley crop. He had the necessary funds.

When Ruth returned to Naomi, she brought with her another gift from Boaz – six measures of dried, threshed barley. He didn't want Ruth to return empty handed. When Naomi received the gift and heard from Ruth what Boaz had said, she had the confidence to tell Ruth that Boaz wouldn't rest until he had finished the business transaction that very day.

On the day in question, Boaz positioned himself at the gate where commerce was enacted. He was early for the meeting, arriving before the "nearer" kinsman. He came prepared with a plan and was armed with information, both factual and legal, that gave him a superior negotiating position. Boaz had the reputation and relationships needed to get ten men of the elders of the city to sit down and be witnesses to the transaction as it was negotiated. Once the negotiation forum was established, he made his first move.

Boaz indicated that he was ready, willing, and able to buy back the land from the person to whom Elimelech had sold it. He told the nearer kinsman that if he wanted to redeem the land, that was fine, but he needed to know so he could redeem it if the nearer kinsman wasn't interested. Correctly anticipating the response from the nearer kinsman that he would redeem the land, Boaz was prepared. It was time to play his trump card.

Boaz had a knowledge of Jewish law, and it appears that he may have also had some knowledge of the nearer kinsman's family situation. Armed with that information, Boaz informed the man that if he was going to redeem the land, he would also have to marry Ruth. Biblical scholars refer to this as "levirate marriage". It wasn't just about acquiring the land. It was also about raising up heirs for the one who had died and providing an inheritance for them.

Upon hearing this, the nearer kinsman bowed out of the transaction. Redeeming the land would have meant purchasing it and giving it back to Naomi, and then producing an heir for Elimelech and his deceased son. That land would ultimately pass to that future-born heir. The nearer kinsman probably had other children and didn't want to mar his own inheritance or complicate his own estate plan, especially by marrying a Moabite. Any offspring would be treated as unworthy by his older children. Under the law of Moses at that time, the stigma of having a child with a gentile would have lasted for generations.

In the presence of the ten witnesses, he transferred the right to redeem the land to Boaz. From a multi-generational perspective, Boaz understood that the land would be given to Naomi and Ruth, and that by marrying Ruth and having a child with her, that child would inherit everything Boaz had, including the land he had just bought back for Naomi. Boaz was investing for the long term, not in some get-rich-quick scheme.

The business transaction was consummated by the nearer kinsman removing his shoe and giving it to Boaz in the presence of the witnesses. This custom arose from the fact that real estate was possessed by treading on it with the sole of one's foot. Handing another your shoe symbolized the transfer of that property or the right to it from one party to the other. The business transaction was accepted, and people complimented and blessed Boaz and Ruth. The future for them had just changed dramatically! Boaz bought back the land and married a willing bride.

Once again, we can extract business principles from this exchange. Boaz was aware of and prepared for the situation even before Ruth came to him. He had the tactical information needed regarding this man who was in a superior legal position to his, and this allowed him to neutralize that man's advantage. Boaz used his knowledge of the situation, his choice of words, and the right timing to achieve his desired end result.

How can I apply this to my business?

Having just money and no knowledge is a recipe for failure in business and real estate investing in particular. Having knowledge without the ability and skill to use it is just a form of mental entertainment.

The transaction between Boaz and the nearer kinsman serves as a powerful example of strategic planning, foresight, and execution in business. Boaz didn't rely solely on his wealth; he combined his financial resources with deep knowledge, tactical preparation, and an understanding of the customs and laws that governed the situation. This enabled him to achieve a favorable outcome not just for himself, but for Ruth, Naomi, and their futures as well. His actions demonstrate the importance of being informed, prepared, and strategic when making critical business decisions.

For business owners, this serves as a reminder that planning for the future is essential, and what you do today can significantly impact not only your business but also your personal life and the lives of those around you. A well-thought-out plan that takes into account legal, financial, and market dynamics can help you navigate complex situations and secure the best outcomes. Just as Boaz was prepared for the negotiation, business owners need to anticipate potential challenges and opportunities and equip themselves with the right knowledge and skills to act decisively.

1. **Inflation** - The one factor that all business owners must constantly be aware of is inflation, whether you are doing business in an economy facing stagflation and growing government regulation or inflation and decreasing government regulation. At the time of this writing, the federal debt that is acknowledged is more than $35 trillion. That is a staggering sum of money, and it means the federal government is going to continue to inflate the U.S. dollar to shift many of our financial indiscretions to other nations and mask the financial irresponsibility in Washington, DC. The truth is that inflation is

going to be a fact of life. Some would argue that about half of all dollars in circulation today have been created in the last four years, which explains why so many things have doubled in price.

2. **Demographics -** Business owners must also be aware of shifting demographics. Most of the baby-boom generation will be completely retired in the next 5-6 years. This is going to change how they invest, how they shop, and where they live, which will fundamentally reshape the face of America.

3. **Reserves -** The increase in interest rates over the last couple of years has taught small business owners that they cannot count on quick and easy lines of credit from banks and other lenders, so they need to have their own deep wells of reserves. When something unexpected came up, Boaz didn't have to go to a bank and go through a lengthy loan application process to have the money to redeem Naomi's land. He was able to reach into his reserves and conclude the business transaction the same day.

4. **Essential products and services -** Just as Boaz's wheat and barley crops were essential to the economy and human existence and offered a variety of uses, business owners would do well to offer goods and services that are essential to everyday life and the economy as a whole. During challenging economic times, people will focus on the essentials – shelter, food, and transportation.

There is another thing, however, that people will look for when things get really tough, as we learned from the marketing of the game Monopoly during the Great Depression. For a small sum of money, people will look for ways to escape from their current reality. Folks today will look for cheap online access to things like movies rather than go to a theater. They will look for things that give them hope and happiness. If the product or service your business offers isn't considered "essential", make sure it offers hope or happiness.

The key is to think long term. When making a decision, ask yourself what that decision will mean for your business in 20 years. If the answer is little or nothing, then the decision is not that big of a deal; but if you realize the decision has long-term implications on your business, it needs to have a lot of thought and planning put into it to properly frame things. This is particularly true for real estate investors who buy properties and then hold them for 10 or 20 years or more.

Failing to plan or lacking the necessary insights can lead to missed opportunities or costly mistakes that could jeopardize not only your business but also the financial security of your family. Conversely, having a strategic approach and the ability to act at the right time can open doors to new ventures, protect your assets, and create a legacy for future generations. The decisions you make today shape the trajectory of your business and the well-being of those who depend on its success. As Boaz's story illustrates, preparation, knowledge, and strategic action are the cornerstones of long-term success in business and life.

Applying Boaz to Generational Wealth:
Rob Anspach Interviews Jeff Watson - Part 1

Rob Anspach: Hey, this is Rob Anspach, and welcome back to another edition of *E-Heroes*. For those keeping track, this is episode 308. I talk about legacy a lot, but my next guest helps investors think about legacy in a much broader sense—not just for the moment, but in terms of generational wealth. That's something we all need to be thinking about, whether we're entrepreneurs, business owners, or even part-time investors. It's not just about today's investments; it's about the future. So, I'm honored to welcome Jeff Watson. Glad to have you here, Jeff.

Jeff Watson: Rob, it's a tremendous honor to be here with you, and wow, episode 308! I have to say, that's some divine serendipity. And here's why—308 is the caliber of a long-range bullet, and today, we're going to be talking about some long-range concepts. It's funny how things line up like that, isn't it?

Rob Anspach: I love that connection. I've gone over a lot of your work, and we've had some great conversations before. It seems like in today's world, people rely too much on technology for investing. They let algorithms make decisions for them, but those algorithms don't understand what you really want when it comes to building a generational legacy.

Jeff Watson: Algorithms are a terrible replacement for thoughtful, deliberate investment planning—especially when you're thinking on a 20-year or, better yet, a three-generation time horizon. That's something you and I have been working on with the book I'm writing, *Boaz on Business*. When you dive into the story of Boaz in the Book of Ruth, you see that he wasn't just making decisions for himself—he was thinking three generations ahead with the real estate purchases he made. That kind of forward-thinking is profound.

Rob Anspach: Right. When you go back to biblical times, we're talking thousands of years ago.

Jeff Watson: Exactly.

Rob Anspach: Trying to get people to grasp that mindset today is tough. When you talk about planning 20, 30, or even 100 years ahead, people get lost. They don't understand the depth of that kind of thinking.

Jeff Watson: No, they don't. It's just not part of the modern mindset.

Rob Anspach: For me, my books are part of my legacy. They represent my knowledge and how I help others shape their own legacies. But when it comes to investing, people often get distracted by shiny objects.

Jeff Watson: Oh, they're not just distracted—they're completely obsessed with those shiny objects. It's like a squirrel chasing after a bouncing ball, darting around and getting nowhere. I focus on making decisions that will benefit my grandchildren and beyond. I often think about how I want my grandkids to talk about me to their own grandkids. I want them to say, "Papa Jeff taught us this," or "Papa Jeff did that for us so we could do this for you." I have two granddaughters right now—one is three, and the other just turned one. We celebrated her birthday last Friday. Even while I'm spending time with them, I often get calls about real estate deals closing, and sure enough, I had another one close that day. It's all about long-term, multi-generational investing. I use real estate as the vehicle to achieve that. I'm strategic in my approach, and I'd love to dive into that mindset with you today.

Rob Anspach: You know, I learned a lot from my grandfather. He was an investor too—real estate, businesses, you name it. And the thing is, he only had a sixth-grade education, but he made more money than some people with master's degrees. I remember sitting in his office as a kid, maybe seven or eight years old, just watching him. It was like everyone else was playing checkers, but he was playing chess—always thinking several moves ahead. But later in life, he developed Parkinson's, and after he passed, everything he built was handed to the next generation. Unfortunately, they didn't understand the legacy he had created, and everything was sold off. It was hard to watch something so powerful slip away.

Jeff Watson: There's a significant trend happening right now, and the numbers don't lie. We're in the midst of the largest transfer of wealth in history. We're talking about trillions of dollars moving from one generation to the next as the pre-baby boom and baby boom generations pass on their assets to their children. But here's the thing—without careful, strategic planning, that wealth can become more of a curse than a blessing. Without guidance, it can fuel enabling, addictive, or wasteful behaviors. For me, as a long-term investor, it's not just about accumulating assets; it's about sharing the knowledge, teaching the mindset, and helping people develop the thought processes needed to set multi-year goals. I've got kids in their twenties who are already beginning to set multi-year goals in their lives. They'll say, "I'm going to do this, and it's going to take two or three years." That's where it starts. Then as they transition from their twenties to their thirties, I can get them to think about 10-year goals. Eventually, they'll be thinking in 20-year increments. It's a process—a shift from this instant-pot, microwave culture to a slow-cooker mindset, letting things develop over time.

Rob Anspach: You were in Europe recently, and I'm heading there in October. One thing that really strikes me is how, in many European countries, people inherit homes that have been in their families for 200 or 300 years. In the U.S., the average homeowner stays in a house maybe 15 years.

Jeff Watson: Actually, it's even less than that—statistically, the average is around seven years. It's crazy. When you're in Europe, you'll see the difference. I visited a restaurant where the current owner had inherited it from her parents, and they were using her grandparents' recipes. That's three generations of legacy right there. And the service, the food—everything was amazing. There's so much love, respect, and dignity in the way they maintain those traditions.

Rob Anspach: Speaking of recipes, most people think of food when they hear that word, but investing has its own set of recipes, too. You show people step-by-step how to build wealth, like following a recipe. But a lot of folks get bored or distracted—they lose patience and stop following the steps.

Jeff Watson: Exactly. The allure of shiny objects and the desire for instant gratification often derail people from following the "recipe" for success. Let me give you two examples. First, let's look at Boaz in the Book of Ruth. When we're introduced to Boaz, he's already a wealthy man, but his actions are a masterclass in business strategy. In chapters two, three, and four, we see how he makes deliberate decisions—specifically, when he buys a piece of real estate that a relative had sold. He wasn't buying it for himself; he was thinking of Naomi, the widow of his relative, Elimelech. But he didn't stop there. He was also thinking about Ruth, Naomi's daughter-in-law, and how the land would benefit her. Boaz sealed the deal by marrying Ruth, and their son, Obed, inherited everything. That's three generations of wealth transfer—from Naomi to Ruth to Obed. And here's the kicker: Obed became the grandfather of David, the greatest king in Israel's history. David, as a shepherd boy, had access to knowledge that most commoners didn't, thanks to the wealth and foresight of his family. That's the legacy Boaz helped create.

Rob Anspach: That's an amazing transformation.

Jeff Watson: Exactly! And it all started with Boaz's strategic thinking. Generations from now, people will still be talking about the decisions you make in business, marketing, and dealing with the challenges that come your way. That's the legacy you're building right now.

Rob Anspach: And you're traveling all over the country teaching people—that's your "scroll." You're spreading the wisdom of how to live and invest like Boaz, and I think that's incredible.

Jeff Watson: One of the things I love teaching is how to take retirement accounts—those long-term investment vehicles—and move a portion into a self-directed account. That allows you to invest in alternative assets. These can be loans, real estate, or even syndicated apartment complexes. Some of the complexes I'm involved in, I'm thinking of them with my grandkids in mind. I was sharing this with a potential investor today: I've invested in a 153-unit apartment complex near a major university in Ohio, and my grandkids will eventually make decisions about that property. This isn't a short-term deal. We're in this for the long haul, because it's about generating cash flow and long-term wealth appreciation. If I had to sum up my investment approach, I use those two principles—cash flow and wealth appreciation—as my yardsticks for evaluating deals. That's how I know if it's a good long-term, strategic investment. And yes, I travel a lot, teaching about self-directed retirement accounts. These accounts offer more control and predictability than stocks, bonds, mutual funds, or ETFs. I'm not saying you go all-in on alternatives—you diversify. But I like putting some money into deals where I can lend it out, get a double-digit return, and know it's secured by real estate in case things go sideways.

Rob Anspach: Yeah, I know what you mean. Twenty years ago, I put some money into long-term stocks. I'm not a huge fan of stocks, but I dabbled. The long-term strategy always wins out. But people panic. They see their money in the market for two weeks, and if it dips, they freak out and want to pull it out.

Jeff Watson: Exactly. People expect instant results. But long-term strategies are what pay off. Not every individual investment will be a winner, and that's why I lean on index funds when I'm in the market. I've got 500 bets spread across the pool, and I know what the 70-year track record looks like. Now, we always have to give the disclaimer—past performance doesn't guarantee future results—but if American culture continues evolving, I'm confident we'll be okay for the next 20 years.

Rob Anspach: Wow, that's a solid mindset.

Jeff Watson: It is. But let me share my regret from my early days of investing. I was too focused on transactions in my first 10 years as a real estate investor—buying, fixing, flipping, running rentals, and selling them off as soon as I had a profit. I was short-sighted. Now, I buy to cash flow and appreciate. It's repetitive and boring, but it works. I might take some equity out to put into another project, but I don't heavily leverage things. These are long-term holds. And when I sell, I trade up.

Rob Anspach: A lot of real estate investors forget about the power of depreciation.

Jeff Watson: Oh, yeah. The tax benefits of long-term real estate depreciation are fantastic. But you have to be strategic. Depreciation is essentially a low-interest loan from the IRS unless you make your next move carefully. If you're strategic, you can use a 1031 exchange to defer taxes or consider a deferred sales trust if you're dealing with a large enough amount—around $10 million, in my opinion. Alternatively, you could roll it into a Delaware statutory trust if you're unsure about the next steps. But typically, you just 1031 into a better property, and keep doing that. The ultimate goal is to pull off a "Steinbrenner," meaning you die with little to no estate taxes, and your heirs benefit from the stepped-up basis.

Rob Anspach: Right, that's how it's done properly.

Jeff Watson: Exactly. A lot of people aren't comfortable thinking about this, but I invest in real estate with my own mortality in mind. I'm not just investing for me—I'm investing with the intention of passing it on to my kids.

Rob Anspach: That's the right mindset.

Jeff Watson: The big question for me is: have I set things up so that my kids can handle the bumps and surprises after I'm gone? Have I taught them to be long-term thinkers, planners, and investors? Have I lived out those principles for them to see? Because, as they say, more is caught than taught. A few years ago, I had a significant health scare, and one of my kids said to a friend of mine, "What would happen if I lost my dad with everything he's got going on?" My friend told them, "You'd call me and the other people he works with, and we'd guide you through it."

Rob Anspach: That's where due diligence comes in. A lot of people don't fully understand what they're getting into with investments.

Jeff Watson: You're absolutely right. It goes back to the shiny object syndrome—people get distracted by something new and exciting without looking deeper. For those who need a visual, think of the squirrel from the *Ice Age* movies chasing the acorn. That's what too many investors do. They get caught up in the "sizzle" without examining the "steak." I look beyond the surface to see who's involved, what the property is like, the paperwork, the operations, and the track record. I want to know what they've done right, but more importantly, I want to hear what they've done wrong and how they learned from it. If they can't talk about their mistakes, that's a huge red flag.

Rob Anspach: Startups are one of the biggest shiny objects. People get excited, thinking they've found the next Google or Facebook, but the returns are often lousy.

Jeff Watson: It's either that or restaurants, which also have notoriously bad returns.

Rob Anspach: Speaking of investments, what inspired you to write about Boaz?

Jeff Watson: It came out of a tough period in my life after an unwanted divorce. I was older, but I'd managed to keep some money through the divorce, and I thought, "Who do I need to become to be a desirable partner in the future?" As I was studying the Bible, I found myself drawn to the story of Boaz in the Book of Ruth. Yes, it's a love story, but I started to see it as a manual on how to run a well-structured, successful business that generates both income and wealth.

Rob Anspach: It's not a story that's told often, at least not in Catholicism or some other Christian denominations. It's more of an Old Testament story that might get more attention in the Jewish faith.

Jeff Watson: And there are some powerful business principles in Boaz's story. He was a generous man, and I've seen that every one of my mentors who has generosity at their core has been blessed in their business. Generosity, integrity, and clear communication are key components of a successful business. If there's one issue I would hammer on today, it's the lack of clear communication. So many businesses create confusion and chaos because they're not clear in their messaging—to customers, colleagues, or employees. But when communication is clear, everyone is on the same page, and that's when the business moves forward like a well-rehearsed marching band playing in unison.

Rob Anspach: I agree. And in today's world, especially after Covid, people don't feel safe or know who to trust. As entrepreneurs, we have to build that trust. A lot of that comes from being generous, though I admit, I'm not always generous. Sometimes I'm selfish.

Jeff Watson: And that's okay. There are times when you need to protect your time and energy. Otherwise, you'd never get anything done.

Rob Anspach: True. But I see how generous you are with your time, traveling and educating people. It amazes me how much energy you put into sharing these important messages.

Jeff Watson: I appreciate that. There are two messages I'm passionate about sharing: hope, confidence, peace, and freedom. Those four words guide everything I do in business and in life. I want to give people hope that they can change their family's financial future with the right tools and strategies. Confidence comes from my faith—God has never failed me, though I've failed Him plenty of times. Then, there's peace, which comes from doing business the right way, with clear communication and good structure. That peace leads to freedom—freedom of time and financial ability to do the things I want to do. I'm passionate about teaching people how to grow self-directed retirement accounts and advocating for political change that protects our business freedoms. I've done a lot of successful lobbying over the years in Ohio, on Capitol Hill, and now in Texas. One of my clients recently nailed it in front of the Texas legislature with a script I helped him with. These efforts aren't just about making money—they're about building a legacy for future generations. Because if we don't stand up for our freedoms, no amount of wealth will matter.

Rob Anspach: Absolutely.

Jeff Watson: If we're told who we have to rent to, when we have to rent, and at what price, that's a fast way to destroy the real estate portfolio I'm building for my family. We have to protect those freedoms.

"Generosity, integrity, and clear communication are key components of a successful business."

Chapter 5: His Legacy

"Boaz's legacy stretched far beyond his own lifetime, leaving a profound impact on his descendants, including King David."

"Legacy" can be defined as the long-lasting impact of decisions and actions that were made in a person's life. When Boaz looked out on his fields during the harvest and saw all the reapers, servants and gleaners, he recognized the responsibility he had toward all those people. He realized that his business and its success or failure had daily as well as long-term impacts on the lives of many others.

Remember the business deal that Boaz made regarding Naomi's land and how he handled that transaction with the nearer kinsman? At the end of the book of Ruth, we see that the community rejoiced over the union of Boaz and Ruth and the restoration of the land to Naomi. Boaz had made a very shrewd real estate investment. The actions he took and the strategies he employed brought results that benefited many in the community. His long-lasting impact – his legacy – touched more than just his own life, business, and family.

Boaz's legacy stretched far beyond his own lifetime, leaving a profound impact on his descendants. He lived in a time of significant challenges—famine, social unrest, and the everyday uncertainties of agrarian life in ancient Israel. Despite these obstacles, Boaz demonstrated resilience, wisdom, and a deep faith in God. His steadfastness in adversity, along with his commitment to integrity, positioned him as a respected leader in his community. These traits would have been well known to his descendants, passed down as family stories of perseverance, divine favor, and wise decision-making.

When David, the great-grandson of Boaz, penned the words to Psalm 1, I wonder if the stories he had heard about his great-grandfather influenced his thoughts. The stories of Boaz would have provided David with a rich heritage of faith and practical wisdom, reminding him that a righteous life is one that endures hardship, relies on God's provision, and chooses to bless others. When David wrote about the blessed man being like a tree planted by the rivers of water, his words resonate with the life Boaz lived—a life rooted in faith, nourished by God's guidance, and fruitful in its outcomes.

Boaz's life stood as a testament to the enduring truth that those who delight in the law of the Lord, as David wrote, will be like trees planted by the waters, steadfast and fruitful through every season. The life of Boaz testified to the fact that when you align your actions with godly principles, blessings follow, much like the steady, life-giving flow of a river that sustains a flourishing tree.

David's admonition in Psalm 1 to avoid the counsel of the ungodly and not stand in the way of sinners echoes Boaz's discerning nature. Boaz did not simply follow the ways of the world; he made choices that honored God, even when those choices were countercultural. In a time when it was common for landowners to exploit vulnerable workers, Boaz protected and provided for them, particularly Ruth. His actions were not driven by profit alone but by a higher moral compass that prioritized righteousness and compassion over personal gain.

Boaz's decision to redeem Naomi's land and marry Ruth was not just an act of kindness; it was a strategic and courageous move rooted in his understanding of God's law and his commitment to doing what was right, even when it involved personal risk. This willingness to act with integrity, to be generous and kind, and to stand up for what is right would have been values cherished and retold within the family, influencing David's view of leadership and godliness.

David's deep sense of justice, his respect for God's law, and his own desire to lead with integrity were also likely influenced by the stories he grew up hearing about Boaz. Boaz's legacy was not one of earthly wealth alone but of spiritual wealth—a life that bore good fruit, both in the fields of Bethlehem and in the hearts of those who followed him. It is not hard to imagine David reflecting on Boaz's example when writing the Psalms, as he sought to lead his own life and kingdom in a way that honored God.

Boaz had endured a large-scale famine, political uncertainty, and all the other risks of being an investor and a grain farmer. He had persevered, and God had richly blessed him. The connection between Boaz's life and David's writings in Psalm 1 provides a compelling example of how values and faith can be passed down through generations, shaping not only individual character but also the destiny of an entire family line and nation.

How can I apply this to my business?

There is a cultural influence telling entrepreneurs that they need to build businesses designed to serve only themselves. That is only looking at one side of the coin. While a business should be operated to serve the owner and their family, it should also be run in such a way as to be mindful of the impact it is having on the employees and their families. Everyone who is earning a paycheck from you is using that money to take care of themself and possibly a spouse, kids, or even parents.

It's important that your business is run properly so it can provide stability in the lives of your employees, even in chaotic times.

This responsibility to your employees should not be taken lightly. It should guide the actions and decisions made both in the business and in the personal lives of those who own the company. Problems in the personal life of a business owner can impact a business and cause it to struggle. This creates a ripple effect that is felt by the families of the employees.

So, time passes, and your years of hard work have allowed you to build a successful business. It's time to step back a bit and enjoy some of the fruits of your labor. When you've built a business to the point where it can fund the lifestyle you want, don't make the mistake of totally checking out of the company when it comes to the day-to-day operations. Simply drawing a profit distribution with no oversight on what's happening in your business is setting yourself up for massive trouble.

I have no issue with the owner of a business taking a vacation every month if they want, as long as business income and situations permit, but the legacy they desire for their heirs and employees demands vigilance over their assets. There is an element of a fiduciary duty that a business owner has to themself and to their employees. A business owner needs to stay in touch with what is happening in the company so that the revenue being generated by the employees isn't being overly consumed by the owner, who is no longer doing anything to generate that income, to the detriment of all involved with the business.

Just as Boaz impacted those in the community, business owners today should want to leave a legacy that impacts more than just those in their little circle.

What is your business doing to benefit your community?

For those of you who are real estate investors, is it your goal just to see how much money you can make for yourself and your business, or is it your desire to improve your community with the work you do?

When a real estate investor can take on a project such as a beat-up, rundown apartment complex or an ugly house and turn it into a place where people want to live, it is something for which others in the community can be grateful. With good planning and execution, real estate investors can make huge differences in communities that result in decreased crime and overall improvement in the neighborhoods, all while earning a profit for themselves by generating ongoing, consistent, monthly cash flow. Now that's what I call a win-win for everyone!

As business owners and leaders today, we can draw inspiration from Boaz's story, recognizing that our actions, decisions, and values do not just affect us—they ripple through generations. Building a legacy of integrity, faith, and perseverance can impact our families and communities in ways that we may never fully see, much like Boaz's influence on David. Just as Boaz stood firm in his faith, we too can strive to be deeply rooted, allowing our principles to guide us through the challenges we face, bearing fruit in due time for the benefit of those who come after us.

Applying Boaz to Generational Wealth:

Rob Anspach Interviews Jeff Watson - Part 2

Rob Anspach: The other day, one of the political candidates proposed giving people a certain amount of money as a down payment on a house. And I thought, hold on a second—I had to scrimp and save to buy my first house. I actually made a deal with the owner where she financed it for the first year, and then I refinanced once my equity increased. People can get creative like I did. Just handing them money for a down payment isn't going to help in the long run.

Jeff Watson: Let me give you a real-life example of that. I had a long-term rental property in Cleveland, Ohio, near a major trauma hospital, Metro Health Medical Center. It's one of the top trauma centers in the country. The hospital wanted to stabilize its workforce and offered a $10,000 assistance bonus to any employee who bought a house within a certain radius of the hospital. When I had to sell my property due to the divorce, guess what happened? That $10,000 got factored into the price of the house because all the offers were coming from hospital employees with that bonus money.

Rob Anspach: Right, and then those buyers, relying on that "free" money, suddenly can't afford the mortgage payments.

Jeff Watson: Exactly. Here's the thing—if someone's thinking about buying a house right now, don't wait for the market to crash like it did in 2008-2012. That's not going to happen again. You need to buy now because interest rates are starting to drop, and prices are already ticking up. A few people in my network told me just last week that the market has shifted. There was a bit of a slowdown over the summer, but things are picking up again. My advice? Get a house under contract now, and maybe wait a bit to lock in your rate, but don't delay. I expect we'll see the Fed cut rates soon.

Rob Anspach: When my parents bought their first house in the 1970s, the interest rate was between 12 and 14%. It was high, but they understood that in eight years, the equity would grow beyond what that interest cost them. And sure enough, when they sold it, they upgraded to a new house with a much lower interest rate. Sometimes you just have to ride it out.

Jeff Watson: Exactly, you ride it out. When I underwrite deals, I use a 9.9% interest rate. If the property can support that, it's a good deal. Whether this statement ages well or poorly, we'll see, but I expect rates to come down a bit, inflation to tick back up, and then rates to rise again. I think in two years, regardless of who's in the White House, we'll be looking at higher interest rates and higher inflation than we have today.

Rob Anspach: Yeah.

Jeff Watson: They keep tweaking the way they measure inflation to make it look better, but the reality is, we're in for rising rates and rising inflation in the coming years.

Rob Anspach: One thing that's important to me is making sure my kids don't fall into financial debt. I see credit card interest rates hovering around 30% these days, and there's no way anyone paying the minimum balance is going to get ahead. Personally, I put everything on a credit card, but I pay it off at the end of the month. I get the rewards, the points, and I've never paid a dime in interest. That takes discipline. And as an investor, you need discipline too. You can't let yourself get distracted by the next shiny deal. Sometimes, you've got to stick to the course.

Jeff Watson: Absolutely. And most people don't think about the transactional costs in real estate—closing costs, commissions, taxes, and then what's left after rolling into the next deal. It's often not worth it. My strategy is simple: I buy, hold, pay it down, and let it appreciate. Then, I'll work with a private lender to borrow against some of that equity, but I don't exceed 50% loan-to-value (LTV). I use that borrowed money to invest in the next deal that will cash flow and appreciate. It's a snowball effect, but I avoid aggressive debt. I've been down that road before. In 2008, I nearly got wiped out. I don't want to relive that—like watching *Titanic*, we know how it ends every time. People keep saying, "This time is different." No, it's not. You still have to manage taxes, insurance, inflation, and interest rates if you want to be a long-term, strategic investor.

Rob Anspach: So, how can people get in touch with you?

Jeff Watson: Well, the best way to learn about me is through my website, *WatsonInvested.com*. I've got articles, resources, and a free email newsletter that I've been doing for 12 years now—twice a week. Sometimes I talk about events I'm teaching at, and sometimes I just share wisdom. One of my articles is getting republished soon to about 47,000 people. If anyone has a specific question about Roth IRAs or self-directed retirement accounts, they can book an online consult with me through the same portal.

Rob Anspach: You're based in Ohio, but I feel like you're always in Florida.

Jeff Watson: Florida is my happy place. Three years ago, I bought an old, beat-up condo in St. Pete Beach, and after a full rehab, it's become my retreat. I'm planning to make it my primary residence soon.

Rob Anspach: My happy place is Walt Disney World, but unfortunately, I can't make that my primary residence.

Jeff Watson: (Laughs) Yeah, someone else already owns that.

Rob Anspach: Speaking of Disney, here's a man who created an incredible legacy in entertainment, and now it's run by other people.

That's how legacy works. You pass it on to the next generation. Sometimes they make great decisions, and other times they have to bring back the original vision to course-correct.

Jeff Watson: Exactly.

Rob Anspach: Every time I go to Disney, I learn something new—especially about marketing. For me, it's not just a theme park; it's a constant source of inspiration.

Jeff Watson: Disney has perfected the art of transferring money from your pocket to theirs. And they do it in such a way that you actually enjoy the process. It's state-of-the-art.

Rob Anspach: It's all about the experience. When you can build an experience behind your legacy, it transforms more lives than you could ever imagine. The book you're working on isn't just a book; it's going to be an experience. Readers will dive into it, learn history, and envision their future.

Jeff Watson: Exactly. I want them to change their future based on what they've learned from the past in that book. That's my goal. And it's not just Disney creating great experiences. Take Chick-fil-A, for example. I know you love Disney, but I have to say, 99.99% of the time, my experience at Chick-fil-A is fantastic. Last Saturday, you were at a Chick-fil-A, and so was I. Both of us had great experiences, I'm sure. Chick-fil-A is built on solid, biblical business principles, and I study what they do.

Rob Anspach: Chick-fil-A isn't just in the chicken business, huh?

Jeff Watson: Exactly. Chick-fil-A isn't really in the real estate or even the chicken business—they're in the people business. They just happen to sell chicken, but they do it in a way that makes people happy and keeps them coming back. They consistently outsell nearby Wendy's, Taco Bell, and McDonald's, even though they're only open six days a week. Let me share a quick story. I saw an ad recently from two guys trying to sell Steak 'n Shake franchises. Steak 'n Shake has struggled, and in many places, locations near Chick-fil-A have shut down. It all comes back to the experience. That's why I'm now focusing on delivering a better experience in the products, information, and content I provide. If my kids and grandkids have a better experience learning from Papa Jeff, it'll stick with them longer. It's not just about what you teach; it's about how you make it engaging and enjoyable.

Rob Anspach: Exactly. Chick-fil-A has innovated their drive-thru experience so well that it's actually enjoyable. They have people come out to take your order, so you don't have to yell into a speaker. When you pick up your food, they don't use a window—they actually walk out and deliver it to you. It's a different level of service.

Jeff Watson: I've seen that firsthand. Some of their locations have drive-thrus that are three lanes wide. There's a Chick-fil-A in Lakeland, Florida, with a great operator running it, and they move people through quickly. One of my favorite Chick-fil-A operators is in Erie, Pennsylvania—his name's Casey. He runs two stores, both with double-wide drive-thrus, and they keep everything moving. The staff are what I'd call "aggressively friendly," walking beside your car as you move forward, taking your order. It's an exceptional customer service experience.

Rob Anspach: The first time I went to Chick-fil-A, I was struck by how happy everyone was. It almost felt strange because you don't get that level of service at places like McDonald's or Burger King. People there just aren't as friendly.

Jeff Watson: Another chain that comes close to Chick-fil-A is *In-N-Out* on the West Coast. They share some of the same foundational principles—it's family-owned, privately held, and now run by the third generation, just like Chick-fil-A. They also have a biblical foundation, and their drive-thru operates with similar efficiency. It's proof that this kind of model works not just with chicken, but with hamburgers, too.

Rob Anspach: What do you think Boaz would think of Chick-fil-A?

Jeff Watson: I think Boaz would love it. He'd be thrilled to see the level of customer service, the clear organizational structure, and the generosity, like when the staff gives something to a customer for free. Boaz was clear in the Book of Ruth—when Ruth first came to his field, he made sure everyone knew not to harass or mistreat her, even though she looked and spoke differently. He stayed around, had lunch with her, and served her food to show his employees that she deserved the same respect as anyone else. That's the same culture you see at Chick-fil-A and *In-N-Out*. It all starts with leadership.

Rob Anspach: It always starts with the leader.

Jeff Watson: Exactly. Leadership sets the tone for everything.

Rob Anspach: We have a few more minutes left. Any final words of encouragement? Anything you'd like to share?

Jeff Watson: Absolutely. I'm going to share something that I hope comes out right. I've talked a lot about hope, confidence, peace, and freedom today, but there's a fifth word I want to add: *patience.* Patience, in the form of contentment. We've touched on this in our conversation—people are constantly chasing quick fixes and shiny objects, and that's not patience or contentment. Sometimes, especially when you're starting out and struggling, you've got to embrace the struggle. Because once you climb to the top of the mountain, you'll remember how much you grew in the valley. And that will give you a sense of peace, knowing you were content, patient, and did the hard work in the valley while climbing the mountain. And here's the thing—crops grow better in the valley than they do at the top of the mountain. So when you reach a peak, enjoy it, but remember, you're going to face another valley and another mountain to climb. That's the cycle of life. And it's important to teach others that process—how to grow in the valley, climb the mountain, enjoy the journey, and be ready to do it all over again.

Rob Anspach: There you have it, folks. That's what makes Jeff an E-Hero, and someone you can trust.

"Teach us what we need to know,
and don't try to control everything once you're gone."

Reflections

Chapter 1: Wealth & Integrity

In this chapter, we're introduced to Boaz, a man of both wealth and integrity, whose approach to business is deeply rooted in faith and stewardship. Boaz wasn't just a successful businessman—he was a man of character, driven by the principles that shaped his every decision. The way Boaz conducted himself, from greeting his workers to being fully present in his business operations, reveals a model of leadership that emphasizes respect, humility, and accountability to God.

What strikes me most about Boaz is his ability to combine business acumen with generosity. He didn't hoard his wealth; he shared it with others, especially those in need. His interactions with Ruth show us that wealth is a tool to be used wisely, not just for personal gain but to uplift others.

As we reflect on this chapter, I encourage you to think about how Boaz's approach can apply to your business. Are you actively present in your operations? Do you lead with both strength and compassion? And most importantly, how can you ensure that your wealth is not just accumulated but shared in ways that create lasting impact? Boaz's legacy challenges us to do more with what we've been given.

Chapter 2: Diligence & Diversification

Boaz's wealth wasn't just about accumulation—it was about management, foresight, and generosity. This chapter takes a closer look at how Boaz not only maintained his wealth but grew it through tough times. He understood that wealth, whether inherited or earned, requires diligence and diversification to withstand the challenges of political and economic uncertainty.

What stands out to me is that Boaz wasn't passive during the famine. While others sold their land, Boaz stayed the course, using his reserves wisely. He diversified his crops and remained resilient, making decisions that allowed his wealth to grow even in hardship. His story reminds us that during times of uncertainty, opportunity lies in staying vigilant and adaptable.

Boaz also demonstrated the importance of generosity. He didn't just comply with the minimum standards of the law when it came to helping the poor—he went above and beyond. His care for Ruth shows us that wealth is a responsibility, not just a privilege.

As you reflect on this chapter, ask yourself: How are you managing your wealth in times of uncertainty? Are you building reserves and diversifying your assets? And how can you be more generous, ensuring that your wealth positively impacts those around you?

Chapter 3: Risk Management

Boaz's success in business wasn't just about wealth—it was about risk management, leadership, and the value of his team. In this chapter, we see how Boaz understood the importance of protecting his assets and being present in his business operations. His presence at the threshing floor, sleeping near his grain to prevent theft, shows us that being actively involved in key moments of your business can make all the difference.

What I find most compelling is Boaz's understanding of the value of his team. He provided for their needs, ensuring they had the resources to work effectively, and he led by example. He didn't distance himself from the process; he was right there, working alongside his people. This type of leadership creates loyalty, respect, and trust, which are invaluable in any business.

Boaz also understood the importance of organization. His team had clear roles, and everyone knew their responsibilities. This structure not only allowed his business to thrive but also mitigated risk in times of uncertainty.

As you reflect on this chapter, consider how you are managing risk in your business. Are you present at critical moments? Do you value and support your team? And is your organization structured to withstand the challenges that may come your way? Boaz's approach offers timeless lessons in leadership and strategy.

Chapter 4: Continuity

In this chapter, we turn our focus to the future—Boaz's legacy and what it means to build something that outlasts you. Boaz wasn't just focused on short-term gains; his actions were designed to ensure generational wealth and continuity. He understood that true success in business isn't measured by your current balance sheet but by what you leave behind for those who come after you.

Boaz's story is a powerful reminder that our business decisions today impact future generations. His redemption of Naomi's land wasn't just a business transaction—it was a commitment to preserving and restoring family legacy. He wasn't just protecting his own wealth; he was ensuring that his actions benefited his community and future descendants.

For those of us striving to build lasting wealth, this chapter encourages us to think beyond immediate profits. Are we making decisions today that will positively impact our families and communities tomorrow? Are we building businesses that can weather storms and provide stability for the next generation? Boaz's focus on legacy challenges us to take a long-term view of success, to build with intention, and to always consider how our actions will resonate in the future.

Legacy isn't just about what we accumulate—it's about what we leave behind.

Chapter 5: Future Generations

As we come to the final chapter, we delve into the most profound aspect of Boaz's life—his legacy. Boaz wasn't just a wealthy man; he was a man of influence, integrity, and generosity, all of which culminated in the lasting impact he had on his community and future generations. His legacy wasn't built on wealth alone but on the values that defined his life and his business.

Boaz's actions show us that legacy is not about what you take with you, but what you leave behind. His willingness to redeem Ruth and Naomi's family land, his generosity in ensuring the poor were provided for, and his strategic approach to business all speak to a legacy built on kindness, responsibility, and foresight. He understood that the true measure of wealth is found in the lives you touch and the stability you provide for those who follow.

This chapter is a call to think deeply about the legacy we're building. Are we simply accumulating wealth, or are we using it to create lasting value for our families, our communities, and the generations to come? As Boaz shows us, the most enduring legacies are not built on fortune alone but on principles of stewardship, generosity, and integrity.

In reflecting on this chapter, I challenge you to ask: What will your legacy be? And how can you start building it today?

Here's to your legacy!

Thank you for allowing us to bring the lessons of Boaz to you.
It's been our pleasure.

About Eddie, Kira & Rob

EDDIE SPEED – Personal training from the nation's most experienced note buyer!

Since 1980, W. Eddie Speed has dedicated his professional life to the seller financing and non-performing note industry. Over the years, he has introduced innovative ideas and strategies that have positively impacted the way the industry operates today. Eddie founded NoteSchool which is a highly recognized training company specialized in the teaching of buying both performing and non-performing discounted mortgage notes. He is the owner and president of Colonial Funding Group LLC, which acquires, and brokers discounted real estate secured notes. In addition, he is also a principal in a family of Private Equity funds that acquires bulk portfolios of notes. He has been a leader and innovator in the Note Business for over 30 years. He will tell you that those 30 plus years have prepared him for the incredible opportunities of this current real estate market.

KIRA GOLDEN - CEO of Direct Source Wealth.

The desire of Kira and her companies is to help others generate passive income for multiple generations. Kira co-invests with individuals who are looking to generate passive income and a diversified portfolio. She and her dynamic team source and participate in various deals primarily focusing on commercial real estate. They work directly with partners to replace earned income with passive income and create the opportunity to acquire, what is in Kira's opinion, the greatest wealth – quality time doing what you love with whom you love. She has been an active investor since the age of 18, doing it full time for the last seven years. Kira has built a portfolio for herself as well as for her co-investors which includes vacation rentals, large multifamily commercial real estate, and various holdings in start-up companies and alternate ventures.

ROB ANSPACH – Lifelong entrepreneur, marketing strategist, publisher, speaker and podcaster.

Rob is an experienced Marketing Strategist, SEO Expert, Author, Publisher, Speaker and Trust Creator who can transform and monetize your brand.

He's the author of "Social Media Debunked", "Share: 27 Ways To Boost Your Social Media Experience, Build Trust and Attract Followers", "Lessons From The Dojo: 101 Ways To Improve Your Life, Business and Relationships", and the "Rob Versus" series of sarcastic books. Rob is also the coauthor of "Optimize This: How Two Carpet Cleaners Consistently Beat Web Designers On The Search Engines", "The #AskDrA Book Series: Easy & Practical Answers To Enjoying Life As A New Sleever", "No Experience Necessary: Social Media For The Boomers, Gen X-ers & The Over 50 Entrepreneur" and "Power Guesting: Insider Secrets To Profit From Being A Great Podcasting Guest" and contributor to "The

Wise Guys Copywriting Handbook", "Fighting For Truth", "Navigating Hollywood", "The Empathetic Lawyer" and "Unscripted, Unfiltered, Un-Woo-Woo & Un-Guru".

Rob has helped many professionals publish their books which in turn has boosted their authority in their respective niches.

Rob is also host of The E-Heroes Interview Series available on iTunes, Google Play, TuneIn and Apple TV.

Rob works inside corporations across the globe, helping companies generate new revenue and capture online business.

About Jeff Watson

Jeffery S. Watson is an Ohio attorney who has had an active trial and hearing practice for over 30 years. As a trial lawyer, he has a unique perspective on real estate investing, wealth building and asset protection. He has tried over 20 civil jury trials and has handled thousands of contested hearings. Jeff has changed the law in Ohio 5 times via litigation or legislation.

As a real estate investor since 1994, investing in both residential and commercial properties, Jeff has been through multiple market cycles. He currently represents established real estate investors in commercial and residential matters when the transactions involve self-directed retirement accounts. He is a recognized thought leader and innovator in the field of real estate and note investing, wealth building, subject-to transactions, and self-directed retirement account transactions. Thousands of investors have used documents created by Jeff to invest in notes or properties.

Jeff is a nationally-recognized authority regarding regulatory concerns with wholesaling. In his home state of Ohio, he has worked with the Ohio Division of Real Estate and nationally with ARELLO regarding the legality of wholesaling. In 2018, Jeff became a member of the board of directors of Quest Trust Company, a nationally-recognized leader in SDIRA services.

Jeff is general counsel to the National Real Estate Investors Association. Jeff is also general counsel to and a cofounder of Realeflow, LLC, which made the Inc 500 list in 2011. Another of his clients made the Inc 500 list in 2018. He currently advises five different national training or educational organizations with a combined membership of over 200,000 investors. Jeff authors an email newsletter twice a week and maintains a blog at WatsonInvested.com on investing, business and entrepreneurship which are read by over 10,000 successful investors.

From 2010 to present, Jeff has led lobbying efforts in Washington, DC on behalf of real estate investors which has brought about several changes in both government regulation and policy on distressed property purchases and resales. In 2014 and 2015, his efforts on Capitol Hill helped bring about change in the U.S. Tax Code and helped reinstate the Mortgage Debt Forgiveness Act. He also met with FHFA regarding disposition of defaulted notes and mortgages in a bulk format. In 2016, Jeff met with the Consumer Financial Protection Bureau regarding regulating land installment contracts, and he has been working to secure passage of the Affordable Homeownership Access Act in the past three sessions of Congress.

In 2021 Jeff co-led the fight to protect SDIRAs from

harsh restrictions. The Build Back Better bill was amended before the House vote on November 3, 2021, due to these efforts, with the harsh restrictions on SDIRAs removed.

Jeff's efforts to secure reform in the real estate arena aren't just on Capitol Hill. In 2016, he was instrumental in the passage of H.B. 463 amending the Ohio Civil Rights Act to protect landlords from frivolous claims as to "comfort animals". He was the co-creator of the Option Contract Method that revolutionized the short-sale flipping process in 2008. Jeff is one of the most highly-sought-after attorneys in the country when it comes to self-directed IRA investing. He spends much of his time teaching and attending events and representing real estate investors in Washington, DC.

To read what Jeff has to say about investing, entrepreneurship and life, you can go to www.watsoninvested.com.

III**Watson**Invested

The
Jeffery S. Watson
———— Law Firm LTD.

PO Box 604
Conneaut, OH 44030
Phone: 440-599-2827
Fax: 440-599-1836